HIS FINAL DAYS

Lessons from the end of Jesus' life
(and after!)

HIS FINAL DAYS

Lessons from the end of Jesus' life
(and after!)

by G. Tyler Warner

Calvary Chapel Trussville
5239 Old Springville Rd, Pinson, AL, 35126
CalvaryChapelTrussville.com | Office@CalvaryChapelTrussville.com

HIS FINAL DAYS
by G. Tyler Warner

© 2021 G. Tyler Warner
Published by Calvary Chapel of Trussville

5239 Old Springville Rd, Pinson, AL, 35126
CalvaryChapelTrussville.com
Office@CalvaryChapelTrussville.com

ISBN: 978-0-578-86850-9

To Calvary Chapel Trussville –

past, present and future.

CONTENTS

Introduction

His Final Days

John ends his Gospel with this verse: "Now there are also many other things that Jesus did. Were every one of them to be written, I suppose that the world itself could not contain the books that would be written" (John 21:25).

We have four Gospel accounts in the New Testament. Yet aside from the Nativity stories, not one of them spends any time discussing His life prior to His three-year ministry. And within those three years, disproportionate amount of space is given to the very end of Jesus' life.

It's not that the other years of Jesus' life were uninteresting! Quite the contrary, it would seem. But that just makes the four Evangelists' attention to His final days that much more profound. The Holy Spirit seemed to think that we would be alright with fewer miracle stories and parables as long as we did not skimp on Passion week and what followed.

What you're reading now began as a sermon series leading up to Easter. We at Calvary Chapel Trussville had finished a Wednesday-night series on the attributes of God, and were only a few days out from Palm Sunday. So I took that opportunity to teach on the highlights of the final moments of Jesus' ministry. That became a six-part series, and it's still available on our website if you'd like to hear it!

As I was reviewing the notes at the end of that year, I realized that there were some important lessons here, some insights the Lord had given me that I thought were worth repeating. And since I had taught that series in manuscript form (something I never usually do!), the text was just about ready. Seemed as though the Lord had been preparing the way for this little book. That's how I took it anyway, and here we are.

The editing process was a joy to me as I rediscovered some things that I had learned the previous year. I hope you experience that same joy as you read. I decided to add two more chapters – on the cleansing of the Temple and the Ascension – to fill it out a little more. Those two chapters illustrate what you can expect from this book.

The cleansing of the Temple chapter, for example, is very heavy on application and storytelling. The chapter on the Ascension is instructive and doctrinal. The tone and style of each message will be a little different from the others. I hope that gives each part its own flavor and provides a broad range of lessons to be learned.

These studies are not connected by any through-line other than the chronology of the end of Jesus' life and after. So don't look for chapter 4 to reference chapter 1, etc. I've done my best to reduce redundancy so that you don't read the same point twice, but some of that is unavoidable, since everything is so interconnected.

Of course, I could have made this book much longer. I might have spoken about the disputes Jesus had with the Pharisees, or the Olivet Discourse, or His trial in the Garden of Gethsemane. But like John said, there's just too much to include in one little book. As Pilate said to the Jews: "What I have written, I have written" (John 19:22). Believe me, there is plenty here to keep us busy.

I think God intended us to be busy meditating on the final days of Jesus. He used the limited space of Scripture to tell the story in all its richness and fullness – four times! I hope that as you read what I've written here, you will not be impressed by my cleverness or depth of knowledge (or distracted by a lack thereof!). I hope you will be captivated by the story of the Son of God who died for our sins. That the love of His Father will transform your heart, and that His Holy Spirit will fill you up with joy unspeakable. May my name perish from the earth as long as that of Jesus is lifted high!

Above all, if you read this not as a Christian but as a curious seeker, I hope you will hear the voice of God as He draws you to Himself. The end of Jesus' life is not just a tragedy turned to victory, it is the story of how God intervened in the world to save those who would call on His name. If you read this book to the end, you'll hear the Gospel a lot. I urge you to respond to it. And to my brothers in sisters in Christ, pray as you read that this will not just be another book (Ecclesiastes 12:12), but a scalpel in the hand of the Lord to perform open-heart surgery on just one lost soul.

This is the story of the love of Jesus.

This is the story of His final days.

1

Give and Take

The Anointing at Bethany

INTRODUCTION

Holy Week begins on Palm Sunday, but on Saturday night there was an important event that should not be overlooked. That is His anointing by Mary in the town of Bethany. This story is found in all four Gospels, but we will look at the account in the book of John.

At this point in the story, Jesus has nearly come to the end of His long trek to Jerusalem for the Passover feast, where He knows He will be crucified. Immediately before this, Jesus had raised Lazarus, the brother of Mary and Martha, from the dead.

In this story, we see two primary figures: Mary, the sister of Lazarus, and Judas Iscariot, the disciple who would betray his Master not many days later. Each of these lives had been transformed by Jesus of Nazareth, and both were disciples of His – but the motivations of their hearts were very different, and their destinies were inverted images of one another.

Jesus said in Matthew 10:39, "Whoever finds his life will lose it, and whoever loses his life for my sake will find it." We can either be givers or takers when it comes to God. Jesus has commanded us to give our lives away, and He has warned us about what happens to those who cling to theirs too closely. May we all be put to the question by the Holy Spirit: Are you a giver or a taker? If you are a giver, then abundant eternal life will be yours; but a taker is destined for a lonely grave of his own making.

"Six days before the Passover, Jesus therefore came to Bethany, where Lazarus was, whom Jesus had raised from the dead. So they gave a dinner for him there. Martha served, and Lazarus was one of those reclining with him at table. Mary therefore took a pound of expensive ointment made from pure nard, and anointed the feet of Jesus and wiped his feet with her hair. The house was filled with the fragrance of the perfume. But Judas Iscariot, one of his disciples (he who was about to betray him), said, 'Why was this ointment not sold for three hundred denarii and given to the poor?' He said this, not because he cared about the poor, but because he was a thief, and having charge of the moneybag he used to help himself to what was put into it. Jesus said, 'Leave her alone, so that she may keep it for the day of my burial. For the poor you always have with you, but you do not always have me.'" (John 12:1-8)

JESUS INTERVENES IN THE STORY

This is a short story, but a significant one. Other than asides from the narrator, this is the first indication we have that Judas's heart is rotten on the inside. Up to this point, there was no reason to suspect that he was anything other than a faithful disciple like Andrew or Levi. And this is also the redemption of Mary, her act of repentance before the Lord. The last time we saw her she seemed to have lost her faith, and yet here she is at Jesus' feet.

That was where we first met Mary, actually – sitting at Jesus' feet. She lived with her sister Martha and her brother Lazarus. When Jesus came to their house in a small town, Martha worked to be a good hostess, but Mary sat at Jesus' feet to hear him teach. Martha was angry, and ordered Jesus to send her sister back to work where she belonged. "But the Lord answered her," in Luke 10:41-42, "'Martha, Martha, you are anxious and troubled about many things, but one thing is necessary. Mary has chosen the good portion, which will not be taken away from her.'" Mary loved Jesus, and He refused to deprive her of His word.

The Lord had a soft spot in His heart for this little family. They seem to have been poor, and probably young, considering they were unmarried and still living together. Perhaps they saw Jesus as a big brother or a father figure. That is why it stung Mary so badly when Jesus delayed to come and heal her brother when he took sick. By the time Jesus arrived, Lazarus was already dead and buried. Mary didn't even bother to come and greet Him when He arrived. When Martha finally made her go to Him, all she could say was, "Lord, if you had been here, my brother would not have died." It was at this point that Jesus famously wept (John 11:35).

But Jesus raised Lazarus from the dead, and in this story they were celebrating. Mary's doubts had been overcome by the power of Christ, and so she anointed Him with costly perfume in an act of sincere repentance.

Judas, however, did not appreciate what Mary did, and for those of us reading this story, it might surprise us that he would react so strongly. After all, Judas was one of the Twelve. His life had been affected by Jesus no less than Mary's had.

Judas Iscariot had been handpicked by Jesus to be one of the Twelve after a long night of prayer. He went with Jesus everywhere, and would have known Him just as well as any of them. Doubtless, he had had intimate, personal moments with Jesus that no one else had shared. He had seen lepers healed and demons cast out with a word. He had done these things himself in the name of Jesus. He had gone throughout Israel proclaiming the Kingdom and had even baptized other would-be followers of Christ. He was there when Jesus confronted the Pharisees, and Jesus had even saved his life when He calmed the waves with a word.

The lives of both Mary and Judas had been completely transformed by Jesus of Nazareth. They could not have known beforehand that their lives would be devoted to a carpenter from Galilee, but once they met Him, neither could ever be the same again.

It is the same with you and me. Every one of us has been affected by Jesus of Nazareth. There came a moment in your life when you decided that you were going to trust Him as your Savior and serve Him as Lord, probably a series of such moments. You live differently because of the things He said. The routine of your week is built around worshiping Him. You may have even traveled to a foreign country in deliberate discomfort to persuade other people to follow Him. Even if you are not a Christian, you cannot escape the man Christ Jesus. Your entire culture is saturated with His words and His people. But if you are a Christian, all the most significant moments of your life have been stamped with His presence.

How could Judas and Mary disentangle themselves from Jesus? They couldn't. But why would they want to? Jesus had given them purpose and hope. He showed them how to live, and He taught them why life was worth living in the first place. There's no way to untangle the knot that ties you to Jesus, not without causing serious damage. One of these two characters has learned this to be true. The other will have to learn the hard way. And he will not learn until it is too late.

GIVERS AND TAKERS

Although both Mary and Judas had decided to follow Jesus, they had done so for very different reasons. The motivations of their hearts were opposites. Mary followed Jesus with a generous attitude. She kept nothing back from her Lord, she was willing to give Him everything. Judas, on the other hand, was only in it for what he could gain. He never gave Jesus anything, he only took from Him. And because of this difference in their hearts, two lives that appeared to be on the same trajectory were in fact headed for very different destinations.

Mary had always been delighted by Jesus. She snuck away from her duties to sit at His feet, and Jesus could not refuse the genuine love she had for Him. Even though her faith wavered at the death of her brother, she returned to His feet one more time to honor Him as her Lord.

As I said before, Lazarus and his family were not rich people. The fact that Mary had such expensive perfume does not indicate that they were wealthy. Quite the opposite. Judging by the reactions of the guests, this was probably the only thing of real value they had in that house. Nard came from East India. It was difficult to acquire and very expensive. That alabaster jar held twelve ounces, nearly a pint of it, and according to Judas was worth nearly a year's wages. Why would they have had this? It has been suggested that this was in fact Mary's dowry, saved for her wedding day as a financial investment. And she broke it to anoint Jesus' feet.

When that precious alabaster broke, the sound signaled not just the loss of money, but the loss of Mary's prospects as a bride. Without a significant dowry, it would be difficult for her to find a worthy husband. No wonder Judas cried out. But the Lord rebuked him and commended her. Because Mary had finally given everything over to Jesus. She had nothing left to hold back, it was all laid at His feet in a beautiful act of lavish worship.

This is the attitude of a giver. Jesus has called us to give up everything to follow Him, like the disciples who left their nets and Levi his tax table. Jesus said, "The kingdom of heaven is like treasure hidden in a field, which a man found and covered up. Then in his joy he goes and sells all that he has and buys that field" (Matthew 13:44). When we recognize what the Kingdom of God is worth, we do not hesitate to give up everything to go after it.

A giver does not count his money as his own. He sees it only as an avenue to exercise love and knows that every dime he gives away is another shackle broken on his heart. A giver does not count her time as her own. She is not concerned with being amused and satiated every minute of every day because she knows that the greatest joys in life can only come through patience and surrender. A giver does not even count his skills as his own. He is overjoyed that his abilities could be used for something greater than his own material gain, and does not hesitate to use them for the sake of God and His people. Givers will give up anything, because they know that in so doing, they lay up treasures in Heaven, where moth and rust can never destroy (Matthew 6:19-20).

It is difficult being a giver, and many will call you a fool. But as Jim Elliot said, "He is no fool who gives what he cannot keep to gain what he cannot lose." He died in the jungle, slain by the very people he came to help – but not a minute later he came into a reward that made everything else seem dull by comparison. Mary had the same attitude, as she demonstrated here in this story.

Judas was not a giver. Judas Iscariot was a follower of Jesus, but he was only in it for what he could get out of it. Like Ebenezer Scrooge, he weighed everything by gain. When Mary broke her alabaster jar over Jesus' feet, all that greed he had been suppressing erupted in an outburst of fury. And when Jesus rebuked him for it, he had finally had enough.

Maybe Judas began with good intentions, who knows? Perhaps when Jesus called him to be one of the Twelve, his heart was full of loyalty to His Master. He knew that Jesus could work miracles, and he had heard Peter's confession that he was the Messiah. But the soil in which these good seeds had been planted was full of thorns.

We don't know when Judas began stealing from the moneybag, but by now it was an addiction. The first time, he probably broke out into a cold sweat and swore to God on his knees that he would never do it again. But the problem was not one act of thievery, but the heart of a thief. Over long years, he seared his conscience until he thought nothing of helping himself to the gifts generously given to Jesus. And it was no longer enough for him. He wanted Jesus to take power, so that he might have the privileged position that would come with it. He resented Jesus for failing to profit from His ministry, and when he was rebuked for wielding the teachings of Jesus like a weapon, a dark purpose entered his heart.

21

During the Feast of Unleavened Bread, mere days after this story, he went to the chief priests and said, "'What will you give me if I deliver him over to you?' And they paid him thirty pieces of silver. And from that moment he sought an opportunity to betray him" (Matthew 26:15-16). Because Judas could gain nothing more from a partnership with Jesus, he sold Him out for a quick buck.

This is the attitude of a taker. A taker does not love God, he loves no one but himself. A taker will attach himself to Jesus, or the Church, because he thinks there is an opportunity to profit by it, financially or socially or any other way. While David said he would not offer anything to the Lord that did not first cost him something (1 Chronicles 21:24), a taker will not offer anything to the Lord unless he can get something out of it.

A taker sees the pulpit as an opportunity to make money, and they end up just as depraved and ostentatious as any celebrity or Wall Street executive. A taker sees the Church as a social ladder that she can climb. She might be bottom-rung at work, but here she has found people who will admire her. A taker sees the worship team as an outlet for his creative passions, or the seminary as a chance to distinguish himself academically. They may give lip service to the true purpose for these things, much as Judas demanded Mary give to the poor, but in their hearts they are only there to serve themselves. This is why you will often see a taker leave the Church abruptly. If they can get somewhere else what they were trying to get at church: a boyfriend, business connections, or an exciting show, they will leave without giving it a second thought.

In the classic film, *Citizen Kane*, the main character is a fabulously wealthy newspaper tycoon. He has everything he could ever want, but his second wife despises him. They live in the most luxurious home, she wears the finest clothes, but she scoffs at him that it doesn't mean anything. "You never gave me anything in your whole life! You just tried to bribe me into giving you something." That is the heart of a taker. They may work, sing and even preach for Jesus, but it's all for their own sake. And the minute they feel they have milked Jesus dry, they will sell Him out for a few pieces of silver.

THE END OF THE ROAD

Jesus told us to give up everything to follow Him. But isn't that narrow? Why can we not join hands with Him and work together for mutual benefit? Why does He demand, as Andrew Murray called it, absolute surrender? It is because God knows that the heart of a taker will not merely disrupt the life of a local church, but will dig the grave of its owner. The road of selfishness leads through a life of desolation and ends in Hell. But he life of a giver is one of liberation from anxiety and fear. A giver is not owned by anything except Jesus Christ, and they know deeper joys that will only continue forever in Heaven. How you choose to act towards God, as a giver or a taker, will determine both your life and your destiny.

Judas began well, but his selfishness made him a thief, a loudmouth and a betrayer. That's what happens when you live life as a taker. You become a thief. Every goal you pursue, and every relationship you have becomes a matter of possession. You do not want to win that contest for the joy of competition, you want to win so that you can have the trophy. A taker cannot love anyone else, they can only own people, and treat them with contempt once they've conquered them. A taker becomes a loudmouth. They bark orders and they scoff at pure motives. They may think they've got everyone fooled, but their mouth reveals their arrogant heart. And takers are betrayers. A taker will betray any cause or anybody if they can profit by it. A taker only withholds betrayal because they see loyalty as a better investment.

If you live your life this way, you will drive away everything good, and everyone who loves you. Paul said in Colossians 3:5 that covetousness is idolatry. Why? Because covetousness is the worship of oneself. I am on the throne, and everything I do is for myself. All my labor, all my love and all my plans are only for the holy "I" on the throne of my heart. nonchalant

A taker lives their life in wretched indifference, not caring about what happens around him, as long as he is moving up. But there comes a moment in every taker's life when they must face who they are and what they have become. "When Judas, his betrayer, saw that Jesus was condemned, he changed his mind and brought back the thirty pieces of silver to the chief priests and the elders, saying, 'I have sinned by betraying innocent blood.' They said, 'What is that to us? See to it yourself.' And throwing down the pieces of silver into the temple, he departed, and he went and hanged himself" (Matthew 27:3-5).

Judas had a flash of reality. He suddenly realized what he had done, and he went back to try to change it. But it was too late. The friends he thought he had made were not his friends at all, and the silver he coveted no longer held any attraction for him. He had made his life unlivable by betraying everything he loved for his own gain. And Judas took his own life.

I used to work for a junk collection company. Frequently we would be called to clear out hoarder's houses. These places were piled high with trash and filth; they smelled, they were dangerous to navigate, and the people who had filled them up were either full of shame, or desperate to hold on to the mess they had made. They had everything

25

they wanted, but they had nothing worth having. Usually the family was long gone, and no one dared to approach them. People die in those houses, crushed under the weight of their own stuff. It was like that for Judas, and it can be like that for you if you live your life as a taker. You may get what you want in the short term, but all your schemes can only lead to a hollow victory. That kind of person is living in Hell long before they ever get there. "For what does it profit a man to gain the whole world and forfeit his soul?" (Mark 8:36)

But look at what the Lord said about Mary: "Truly, I say to you, wherever this gospel is proclaimed in the whole world, what she has done will also be told in memory of her" (Matthew 26:13). Mary gave up everything to follow Jesus, but she gained so much more.

She had begun with childish faith, excitable and flighty. Then she too was faced with the fact that she would not be able to get everything from Jesus that she thought she would. But she was able to learn from the faith of her sister and brought the only thing of value she had and broke it at Jesus' feet. Every hope and every dream she had was in that bottle – a husband, a home, children. But she gave it all to Jesus, and she gained freedom from those things.

We can become enslaved to the things that we love, and they need not be material things. We can be in love with the past, treasuring it to the neglect of what's right in front of us. We can be in love with the present, unwilling to change the way things are. We can be in love with the future, obsessed with dreams and plans to the point of immobility and selfish greed. And the Lord knows that covetousness corrupts, which is why He tells us to give it all away.

Now we hear that, and we come up with a million good, biblical reasons why we don't need to give up "that" thing. We compare ourselves to Abraham, who sacrificed Isaac in his heart, and that was enough. But we suspiciously apply that only to things that would hurt to give up. As long as we do that, we will remain stuck. Holding on to the way things are (or were, or will be) will keep us in the same sins and struggles. But as fearful as it may be to smash an alabaster jar full of pure nard, that is the only way to salvation. "Those who belong to Christ Jesus," Paul said, "have crucified the flesh with its passions and desires" (Galatians 5:24).

See what Jesus said about Mary: she had gained eternal life! This is true in two ways: First, she had gained an immortal testimony. Her story is in all four Gospels, and has been told in every church around the world for 2,000 years. Her willingness to give up everything for the Lord has been an inspiration and encouragement to countless millions, as it is for us right now.

When you live as a giver, your life becomes a beacon of light in a dark world. You begin to treat people with love and respect, because you are no longer a god in your own heart, but have become a servant of the Living God. Other people see your example and are motivated by it, and everyone around you is liberated from the shackles of self and stuff a little more every day. And God is able to spread the joy of Jesus Christ to the world through you.

But there is a second way that Mary gained eternal life. She gained it the day she called upon the Lord to receive her spirit and she fell asleep. This part is not narrated, but we know that it is true. Because Mary was willing to give up her life in the flesh, she not only found a new abundant life in the spirit, she had a glorious entrance into the joy of her salvation that will last forever and ever. Just imagine the treasures that were laid up for her there! 300 denarii would seem a pittance compared with such eternal riches.

The Lord returns what we give to Him with interest. He is a good Father who will not allow His children to be satisfied with lesser things. He will not stand by and allow us to addict ourselves to the cheap thrills and paltry baubles of this world. He calls us to give up our lives for His sake. Not because He is a tyrant, but because He knows that this is the way to real life, and after that to eternal life.

CONCLUSION

"Whoever finds his life will lose it," Jesus said, "and whoever loses his life for my sake will find it" (Matthew 10:39). Judas, the taker, became a betrayer and a suicide, while Mary, the lavish giver, went on to joy and immortality. Taking from God and living for yourself, sucking the world dry until you make yourself sick, will leave you alone and desolate. Giving to God and letting Him place better things in your open hands leads to eternal life.

And God has not commanded us to do anything that He has not already done Himself. "For God so loved the world, that he gave his only Son, that whoever believes in him should not perish but have eternal life" (John 3:16). Jesus Christ gave Himself up on the cross. And what did He gain by it? You. Me. Us. He despised the shame of the cross for the joy of eternity spent forever with His Bride, the Church (Hebrews 12:2). He offers salvation freely, as a gift to anyone who will receive it by faith.

Takers even bring their attitude to salvation. They think they can take salvation from God. Rather than viewing their sin as a tragedy, it's just a factor in the equation. They want Heaven, not because it means life with Christ, but because it's the only alternative to Hell. So they try to work the Christian system. They'll go to church or tithe or serve or even preach because they think it will gain them eternal life. A Christian taker thinks he's got God right where he wants Him, and now He has to let him into Heaven. He does the bare minimum to secure his ticket to paradise, but he is terribly deceived. Ephesians 2:8-9 says, "For by grace you have been saved through faith. And this is not your own doing; it is the gift of God, not as a result of works, so that no one may boast." A boastful, covetous attitude will get nothing from God on that final Day when every motivation of the heart will be exposed.

But a giver knows that salvation is beyond them. All they can do is throw their life at Jesus' feet and beg for His mercy. And in that moment, as they lose their lives in this world, they find them anew in Christ Jesus.

Let us follow the example of our Lord, and of Mary, his friend and disciple. Give up everything to follow Christ, the treasure is worth it. Spurn the path of Judas Iscariot, and don't be a taker from God. Break the alabaster jar of your life at His feet.

2

Don't Let the Rocks Cry Out

The Triumphal Entry

INTRODUCTION

Palm Sunday is the day we commemorate the Triumphal Entry. This was the "hour" that Jesus repeatedly told His disciples had not yet come, but now the shroud is lifted. The people openly hail Him as King and Messiah as He rides into Jerusalem for the Feast.

But while this was the most glorious day of Jesus' life and the pinnacle of His popularity, we know that it was not to last. Despite the applause of the crowds, Jesus would be flogged, mocked and crucified by the end of the week. We can already see the cracks forming in this story when the Pharisees command Him to silence His disciples, which leads to His famous words about the rocks crying out. Even then, the disciples of Jesus were under pressure from the world to be silent. We face the same pressures today.

Throughout the centuries and around the world, Christians have been shamed, tortured and even killed to force their capitulation and their silence. The world does not understand us, and even hates us because we are not like them. We serve a different King and look for a different Kingdom. Jesus warned us, "If you were of the world, the world would love you as its own; but because you are not of the world, but I chose you out of the world, therefore the world hates you" (John 15:19).

I am concerned that the Church has lost this understanding. Jesus told the Pharisees that it was impossible for Him to silence His disciples, but since then so many have given in to that pressure. Not many years ago, the song "Jesus Freak" made separation from the world a badge of honor for Christians, but I do not think that attitude prevails any longer. Somewhere along the line we started to believe that distinction from the world was a bad thing. It seems now we are more concerned with soothing the misgivings of the world and seeking their approval. But

Jesus said, "Woe to you, when all people speak well of you, for so their fathers did to the false prophets" (Luke 6:26).

Christ told the Pharisees that if His disciples were to be silent, the very rocks would cry out. It's a powerful image, but we tend to view it incorrectly. It's not a poetic description of creation worshiping its Creator. The rocks crying out would be a disaster! It would mean that God's people had failed to live up to the task to which He had called them, that there was no one left to speak. God will be glorified, regardless of the insecurities of Men, even if He must compel the stones of the earth to do it. But by the grace of God, we must not give in to the demands of the world. We must embrace our status as strangers and sojourners and raise the voice of praise – even if we must do so in the cultural wilderness.

"And they brought it to Jesus, and throwing their cloaks on the colt, they set Jesus on it. And as he rode along, they spread their cloaks on the road. As he was drawing near—already on the way down the Mount of Olives—the whole multitude of his disciples began to rejoice and praise God with a loud voice for all the mighty works that they had seen, saying, 'Blessed is the King who comes in the name of the Lord! Peace in heaven and glory in the highest!' And some of the Pharisees in the crowd said to him, 'Teacher, rebuke your disciples.' He answered, 'I tell you, if these were silent, the very stones would cry out.'" (Luke 19:35-40)

THE TRIUMPHAL ENTRY

For the last few weeks, Jesus had been moving south from Galilee through Samaria and Judea to Jerusalem for the Feast of Unleavened Bread. This was one of the mandatory feasts for all Jewish men to attend, ending with Passover on that Friday. As He made His way closer, the crowds grew and grew, with new disciples being added every day from the pilgrims on their way to the capital. Before Jesus made His final descent down the Mount of Olives, He sent two disciples to retrieve a colt, the foal of a donkey, that had never been ridden before. And when He mounted and began to descend to the city, the multitudes erupted.

They cheered and rejoiced and sang "with a loud voice". Imagine the noise of thousands of voices shouting as they came down. It must have sounded like thunder! According to verse 38, they were singing Psalm 118, one of the Psalms of Ascent that was traditionally sung on the road to Jerusalem, rich with Messianic prophecy. The refrain of the people was, "Hosanna!", meaning "Save us!" from verse 25. They threw their cloaks down on the ground, as if Jesus were too wonderful to tread on the bare earth. And John

12:13 tells us that they broke off branches of palm trees and waved them in the air – hence the name "Palm Sunday".

What was so special about this day, and why did the people respond like this? Because in finishing the journey the way He did, Jesus deliberately fulfilled a prophecy from the Old Testament. Zechariah 9:9 says, "Rejoice greatly, O daughter of Zion! Shout aloud, O daughter of Jerusalem! Behold, your king is coming to you; righteous and having salvation is he, humble and mounted on a donkey, on a colt, the foal of a donkey." All the whispers and speculation about who Jesus might be had been building all the way down to Jerusalem. Rumors had filled the land of Israel – and now He comes down the Mount of Olives riding on a colt, the foal of a donkey!

By waving palm leaves, the Jews were calling for revolution. Palm leaves were a national symbol for the Jews, they signified the rebellion of the Maccabees that had finally thrown off Greek rule from Israel. These people saw Jesus coming, and believed that their deliverance from Roman oppression had finally come. And with some good reason: Zechariah 9:8, the preceding verse, says that "no oppressor shall again march over them." So this procession was not so much a spiritual response as it was a patriotic response. The Jews had finally found the man who would lead them to freedom.

Knowing all that, can you understand why the Pharisees were so worried? The Pharisees were an influential group in Israel. They had seats on the ruling council; they understood the present situation. Judea was on its last chance with the Roman Empire. Rome ruled Jerusalem. They had occupied the land for almost 100 years, they had brutally put down every rebellion, they had built the Antonia fortress overlooking the Temple courts, and they had sent the cold-hearted Pontius Pilate to crack down on Jewish unrest. And now here comes Jesus of Nazareth, riding into Jerusalem in a picture ripped straight from the Old Testament. Thousands flock to see Him, they wave nationalistic symbols in the air, and they sing songs of deliverance from oppressors. The Romans were already on guard against the millions that had come to the city for the Feast. Jesus was putting the peace of Jerusalem in danger! And so they told Him to silence the crowds.

The rulers of Israel were concerned with the world and its system. They evaluated threats based on the rules and realities of this world. After Lazarus' resurrection, they had a council about what to do with Jesus where they articulated their chief concern: "If we let him go on like this, everyone will believe in him, and the Romans will come and take away both our place and our nation." (John 11:48). It was with a political justification that they decided Jesus must die.

But Jesus did not operate on the same level as them. All His life and ministry, He refused to be dragged into a political position. He refused to take sides on issues that were not spiritually relevant. He taught His people to live and to think differently than everyone else. That was why He refused to silence His disciples. When He was dragged before Pilate and asked about the Kingdom, He said, "My kingdom is not of this world. If my kingdom were of this world, my servants would have been fighting, that I might not be delivered over to the Jews. But my kingdom is not from the world" (John 18:36).

CITIZENS OF A DIFFERENT KINGDOM

"Not of this world." A Christian is not of this world; he is different, he is separate from everyone else. This is our first point: We are citizens of a different kingdom. Peter would call us "sojourners and exiles" in 1 Peter 2:11. A sojourner is a traveler; an exile is living in a land that is not his own. Both of these terms speak of temporary status. In 2 Peter he would twice refer to his own body as a "tabernacle" or "tent" (2 Peter 1:13-14), a temporary residence. The writer of Hebrews would compare us to Abraham, who left his old home to come to a new one, willing to live as a stranger there while he awaited the promise. He says that people of faith are "strangers and exiles on the earth" (Hebrews 11:13)

"For here we have no lasting city, but we seek the city that is to come" (Hebrews 13:14). You as a Christian are from a different world.

You might say that Alabama and California are two different worlds. We talk differently, we vote differently, we even eat different foods. But this pales in comparison to your status as a Christian. It's more like this: Disneyland (speaking of California) has a show called the Country Bear Jamboree, with singing animatronic bears. Growing up, my favorite number was called "Two Different Worlds", featuring a bear in swim trunks and snorkeling gear singing to his octopus girlfriend. "Two Different Worlds" indeed! That is much closer to what we are talking about.

When Jesus rode to Jerusalem, He had come to herald a Kingdom – but it was not a kingdom of this world, as the people and the Pharisees thought. The world is a kingdom of nations and parliaments and people; they have to face things like war and famine and disease and public opinion. Our Kingdom is not like that. Our Kingdom will be an everlasting Kingdom of righteousness and light. Our Kingdom has not come yet, but it will, and in the meantime we are to live as good citizens of that Kingdom. So we live in the United States of America, we work and vote and raise families, but our hearts are set on the Kingdom that is to come. Heaven is our true homeland.

God's Kingdom has a different set of Laws than the one we live in now. The world has its laws and taxes and government, and that's all fine. It also has its unwritten laws of morality and ideas and behavior. Everyone in this world follows a cultural code. However, we are bound not by the laws of men, but by the law of the Spirit of Christ who dwells in us. We are not overly concerned with the preferences and opinions of men, because we have the truth of God's Word. In the Bible, God has revealed what is right and true, and we follow that standard over any rule the world might throw at us.

Our Kingdom has a different mission. Every country has a strategy, every country has a goal. Maybe they want to reclaim territory or build their economy. Or to spread rights and liberties to as many people as possible. But our mission is different. Our mission was given to us by Jesus Christ Himself: to make disciples and spread the Good News of the forgiveness of sins. Our mission is not charity work or social engineering, but evangelism. The Gospel is our mission.

And of course, we have a different King. Our King is the King of Kings, the Lord of Lords, Jesus Christ the Son of God. We honor our governors and kings, of course. But only because Jesus has told us to. Our ultimate authority is not the president, but the Christ. It is to Him that we have bent the knee and sworn eternal loyalty, no matter what.

To the average listener, this all sounds very weird. It almost sounds treasonous! Some kings and dictators have certainly thought so. But it is the truth. When brought before the council, Peter gave the final word on this issue: "We must obey God rather than men" (Acts 5:29). We have passed out of this world and into the sphere of God's grace, and that compels everything that we do.

With such fundamental differences, we should not expect to be like the world. They believe this world is all there is, we are looking for a heavenly city. They believe the will of the people or the word of the king is law, but we trust the infallible Word of God. They view the problems and struggles of the nation as the top priority, while we go about the mission of evangelism. They serve a king they can see, we worship Jesus Christ.

Because of this, these two groups, the world and the Church, will evaluate situations differently and come to different conclusions. The disciples of Jesus saw the Triumphal Entry as a day of celebration and joy, but the Pharisees could only dread the political implications. Paul wrote to the Ephesians, "You must no longer walk as the Gentiles do, in the futility of their minds" (Ephesians 4:17). We are not operating on the same level. We think and believe differently. And that inevitably leads to conflict. The Pharisees told Jesus to silence His disciples on that day, but Jesus would not listen. The Bible tells us to pray that we may live quietly and go about our lives even in the midst of strong cultural disagreement (1 Timothy 2:1-2). But the world does not always afford us that luxury.

THE WORLD PRESSURES US TO CONFORM

The Pharisees were not content to allow the disciples to have their celebration. No, they stepped in to silence them by going right to the Man Himself. This is our second point: The world pressures us to conform. The Pharisees had done this throughout Jesus' ministry. They questioned Him, they challenged Him, they even tried trap Him in His words and actions. One time they deliberately brought a man with a withered hand into the synagogue to see if Jesus would heal him on the Sabbath day. They were trying to expose Him as a lawbreaker before the people, and to have a legal violation to hold over His head. Jesus got the better of them in that situation (Luke 6:6-11), but they did not give up. In fact, Jesus' days during this following week would be full of religious leaders trying to embarrass Him with difficult questions.

Just look at what they would ask Him in Mark 12:14-17. "And they came and said to him, 'Teacher, we know that you are true and do not care about anyone's opinion. For you are not swayed by appearances, but truly teach the way of God. Is it lawful to pay taxes to Caesar or not? Should we pay them, or should we not?' But, knowing their hypocrisy, he said to them, 'Why put me to the test? Bring me a denarius and let me look at it.' And they brought one. And he said to them, 'Whose likeness and inscription is this?' They said to him, 'Caesar's.' Jesus said to them, 'Render to Caesar the things that are Caesar's and to God the things that are God's.' And they marveled at him."

The people demanded that Jesus view the world their way. They gave him two options, both of which were limited by their material view of the world. But Jesus was able to provide a third answer because He would not capitulate to their pressures.

God's people have always had to deal with the pressures of the world. You remember that Daniel and his companions, Hananiah, Mishael and Azariah, were brought from Jerusalem to the courts of the king of Babylon. They were given new names honoring new gods (Belteshazzar, Shadrach, Meshach and Abednego), new foods and a new education. For a while they were able to insist upon their separation, eating only vegetables and praying only to the Lord. But there came a time in Daniel 3 when Nebuchadnezzar commanded all of his officials to bow down and worship the golden statue he had erected. When the three companions of Daniel refused, it says he "was filled with fury, and the expression of his face was changed against Shadrach, Meshach, and Abednego" (Daniel 3:19). And they were all cast into the fiery furnace.

The world will put up with Christians and their oddities for a while. They are fine with our lame music and our modest dress. They are fine with us tithing and quoting Bible verses on social media and taking Sundays off. But should a Christian speak too loudly about the wrong thing, the clamor will begin to shut them up. I had ancestors in America during the Revolution. They were Moravians and therefore pacifists who refused to fight. You may disagree with that, but it was their firm biblical conviction. They were sentenced to hard labor for daring to take no stance on the issues of the day. The minute things get serious, the knives come out and their countenance towards us changes. Christians were tolerated in Rome until they refused to burn incense to Caesar. Then they were thrown to the wild beasts in the arena.

This is because the world does not acknowledge the existence of the Kingdom of God. We are operating on two different planes, and the world cannot abide that. We may take the issues just as seriously as they do, but since they do not acknowledge the possibility of a spiritual solution, they demand that we act as if we believed the same as they do. Whether they view us as a threat or an insult or an inconvenience, the world has declared our faith to be aberrant. For those who do not agree, there is immense societal pressure to bend the knee.

How does this pressure come? The book of Nehemiah gives us a masterclass on pressure from the world. As Nehemiah led the people to build the walls of Jerusalem, the nations around them tried everything to stop them from succeeding. The Devil only has a few tricks, but they are deadly.

Pressure comes through mockery, like the regional rulers who mocked Nehemiah's work on the wall. "A fox could knock it down!" they cried. I am sure every one of you has been mocked for your faith. When the fellows at work are heading out to the strip club and you say, "No thank you", there are all kinds of blasphemies hurled your way.

It comes through shame, like the tweets and op-eds you see published today. The princes surrounding Nehemiah tried to cajole him into letting them join, calling his integrity into question. Shame can be a powerful tool, especially for young people, and there is no shortage of media pundits and college professors willing to browbeat Christians into submission.

It comes through ostracization, when Christians are not permitted to participate in society because of their faith. Nehemiah's opponents wrote letters to the emperor to have him recalled or at least forced to stop construction on the wall. Christians today, for example, may not hold public office in many Islamic and atheist countries around the world. How long until Christianity itself becomes grounds for being "canceled"?

It comes through outright violence. Nehemiah's rivals tried to lure him to a peace conference where they had set a trap to kill him. In Japan during the Shimabara Rebellion in 1638, Christians were crucified on crosses out past the tide line. They were drowned in agony as the waves came in. Throughout history the Christian has spent as much time in the dungeon and gulag as he has in the seminary or the sanctuary.

And lastly, this pressure can come in the form of infiltration. Nehemiah went home for a time, and when he returned to Jerusalem, Tobiah, one of his most cunning adversaries, had a guest room in the Temple. If we cannot be stopped, the world will try to send activists and false teachers into the Church who care nothing about the message of the Gospel, but only want to further their own agenda through denominational institutions. This is more prevalent than I think many of us would care to admit.

We have been blessed for centuries to live in a nation that permits freedom of worship. But now that the pressure seems to be increasing, we must not panic. Peter said not to "be surprised at the fiery trial when it comes upon you to test you, as though something strange were happening to you" (1 Peter 4:12). That famous verse was in reference not to executions, but to insults! This is the lot of the Christian. We are pilgrims in this world, citizens of a different Kingdom. Jesus said, "It is enough for the disciple to be like his teacher, and the servant like his master. If they have called the master of the house Beelzebul, how much more will they malign those of his household?" (Matthew 10:25). Jesus faced pressure to conform, and you as His disciple should expect no different.

THE ROCKS WILL CRY OUT

When Jesus was confronted by the Pharisees, He gave an interesting reply. "He answered, 'I tell you, if these were silent, the very stones would cry out" (Luke 19:40). This is our third point: When the Church gives in, the rocks cry out. This was the day of Christ's Triumphal Entry, the day that had been foretold by the prophets. There was no chance that God would allow His Son to go un-celebrated on that day. And so Jesus refused to silence His disciples, Rome or no Rome, Pharisees or no Pharisees. If He had, the earth itself would have split open in a mighty roar of praise.

But that would have been a tragedy! Daniel had prophesied the arrival of the Messiah to the day in Daniel 9, Zechariah had prophesied His means of transportation, and the Psalmists had written the songs ahead of time. If the rocks were to cry out, it may have made for a great story, but it would have meant that the Jews had failed to recognize their Messiah. God was going to have praise on that day, but it was not for the rocks to cry out, it was for the people of God.

If we as Christians capitulate to the pressures of the world, the rocks will cry out. What does that mean? That means that if we are silent when God has told us to speak, or if we hide the light of the Gospel under a bushel, then God will find another way to get the job done. God is not dependent upon us! He's going to use angels as evangelists after the Rapture (Revelation 14). If the Church silences itself, perhaps the Lord will send an unforeseen revival to a community that never knew God, raising up new preachers and evangelists from those who never heard the Gospel because of disobedient Christians. God forbid that the rocks ever cry out in our day!

Is it possible for the Church to reach such a point? It certainly is. We can reach a point where we are totally ineffective. We can do this in two ways: First, by failing to live as God has called us to live. Jesus said to "let your light shine before others, so that they may see your good works and give glory to your Father who is in heaven" (Matthew 5:16). Your life is to be a testimony that the Gospel of Jesus Christ means something, that it has transformative power. At every job I have ever had, I have been asked why I speak without cursing. My answer has always been the same:

because I am a Christian and I am not permitted to allow any corrupt speech to come out of my mouth. Despite the taunts I have endured, I have been able to share the Gospel every time. Would you forfeit that possibility to avoid embarrassment? If you cover up everything religious about yourself and do your best to seem just like everyone else, you have neutralized the possibility of Christian witness in your life.

The other way we can become ineffective is if we are silent. Many times the world does not care what we believe as long as we do not talk about it. Christians are great at coming up with so-called biblical excuses why they do not have to speak about the Gospel or the Bible or Jesus Christ. But we talk about everything else that interests us, so are we so reticent about the most important things? The Bible commands you to speak out. In Mark 16:15 Jesus said, "Go into all the world and proclaim the gospel to the whole creation." That was not just for the apostles, it was intended for you! We are to speak the truth in love (Ephesians 4:15), to have an answer for anyone who asks (1 Peter 3:15), we must speak out! We are the prophetic voice in the world, and we cannot allow the world to go to Hell before our very eyes. Surely Jesus has taught us love better than that?

"You are the salt of the earth, but if salt has lost its taste, how shall its saltiness be restored? It is no longer good for anything except to be thrown out and trampled under people's feet" (Matthew 5:13). When the salt goes bad, the meat spoils. When the Church caves in and goes silent, the world rots. In the Middle Ages, the Church grew silent and permitted all manner of barbaric aberrations to be canonized. It took the Lord raising up a "rock" to cry out: Martin Luther, a little German monk, who brought the Bible and the Gospel back to the people. We rejoice at the Reformation of the Church, but that will be forever to the shame of the pastors and teachers who had gone before.

Are we so desperate for the approval of the world that we are risking a similar situation? Some folks preach polls more than the Scriptures. But why do we care what the world thinks? James the brother of Jesus wrote, "You adulterous people! Do you not know that friendship with the world is enmity with God? Therefore whoever wishes to be a friend of the world makes himself an enemy of God," (James 4:4). We should not be interested in the approval of people who do not believe in God, hate Jesus Christ and despise the Bible. We are citizens of different Kingdoms. If we somehow manage to gain their approval, we should stop immediately and find out where we went wrong. "Woe to you," Jesus said, "when all people speak well of you, for so their fathers did to the false prophets" (Luke 6:26).

The Lord refused to silence His disciples. But we have silenced ourselves. If the Church in America and elsewhere does not halt its downward progress, God will be left with no choice but raise up a rock to do the work. When the Church gives in, the rocks cry out. But as my friend RJ used to say, "I don't know about you, but I'm not going to be outdone by a rock!"

WE MUST RESIST

When the Pharisees tried to pressure Jesus to think on their level, He flatly refused. He would not tell His disciples to silence their praise or tone down their worship. Neither should we. This is our fourth and final point: We must resist the pressure to conform. "Go out from their midst and be separate from them, says the Lord, and touch no unclean thing; then I will welcome you" (2 Corinthians 6:17). God has commanded us to be separate from the world. We are sojourners, not citizens; pilgrims, not partners. People will say that we are strange, but we know that we are strangers. "Not of this world."

We are left with only two choices: We may silence ourselves – shut ourselves in the churches and do our best to look just like everyone else – or we can resist. If we fail to fight, we will fade, and I cannot accept that. It is time for us to recalibrate our hearts and our minds and our Instagram accounts to reflect the authority of the Kingdom of God. The odd thing is, everyone from the New York Times to the Disney Channel is telling us to be different and to embrace what makes us special. We love to be unique! So why not lean in to your identity as a Christian? Take joy in being an outsider, because it means you are an insider in the only circle that will ever matter.

You can start by managing your input. We live in a unique time in history when we can decide who we want to listen to, 24 hours a day. There is a superabundance of books, movies, music and television that we can all access any time we like. So curate your influences. You don't need to be listening to music that is going to acquaint you with perverse sexual acts or watching shows that don't teach you anything except how to curse effectively. Fill your mind with the things of God. You have more access to Bible teaching, theology lessons, translations and background knowledge than ever before. Don't waste it for another 10 episodes.

Not only that, we need to work together. It's time for us to reclaim a sanctifying character to our interactions. When we meet together, it should never be awkward to talk about God or His works or His Word. Choose your friends wisely, and don't evaluate Church for its social benefits. The Church needs old and young, rich and poor, all nations, all backgrounds. We must stop separating ourselves into groups just so we can feel comfortable. We are brothers and sisters in Christ. Together, we can provide the right kind of peer pressure for each other.

But ultimately, in order to resist the demands of the world, we have to rest in Christ Jesus. If you cannot strengthen yourself in the Lord, you will have to look elsewhere for validation – always a dangerous thing. But it is not necessary. The Lord has promised to be your all-sufficient Savior. He is your Comforter and your Teacher, your Father and your Friend who sticks closer than a brother. Immerse yourself in the things of God, as Paul told Timothy (1 Timothy 4:15). If you feel like you don't get anything out of the Bible or prayer or Church, then get out of the shallows, my friend! Don't just read a devotional verse, study the Bible. Don't just pray, fast and pray. Don't just go to church when you feel like it, force yourself to go every time, and find some way to volunteer. Dive in deep and you will see wonderful things in the Law of the Lord.

We will never be on the same page as the world. Even if we can agree on certain things, we are looking for a heavenly city, and we are just passing through this one. You must recognize that and accept it. If you find yourself constantly talking down the Church, and explaining away tough passages of Scripture, you may be capitulating to the pressure of the world. You must resist it! How far? To the point of suffering and death, if necessary.

Don't spend your life trying to figure out the minimum commitment needed to follow Christ. There is no minimum commitment. There is only death; taking up your cross to die alongside your Savior. The world needs your voice and your testimony. There are people who can only be saved through your ministry. How can we try so hard to be just like the world, when they themselves are desperate and dying in the despair of sin? Our country today faces widespread depression, pornography and opiate addictions, and the destruction of the family. And we have the solution in Christ Jesus. Take up the mantle that has been handed down to you by the saints who have gone before. It has never been easy to be a sincere Christian, but there have always been faithful men and women in God's Church. Will you be one?

If not, I solemnly warn you today: If you spend your whole life trying to figure out what you can get away with, you may one day find yourself on the opposite side of where you always imagined. The Pharisees loved the Law and claimed to know the Lord. The coming of the Messiah was their greatest hope. But because they could not shake themselves free of the kingdom of men, they found themselves calling for the execution of Jesus with the haunting words, "We have no king but Caesar!" (John 19:15)

CONCLUSION

We are citizens of a different Kingdom. The world pressures us to conform. When the Church gives in, the rocks cry out. We must resist the pressure to conform.

Jesus did not capitulate on Palm Sunday. He did not capitulate at any time during His ministry. And He did not capitulate in the Garden of Gethsemane. When the pressure was on Him to refuse the cross, He said bravely, "Not my will, but yours, be done" (Luke 22:42). He went to the cross and suffered and died, in the ultimate act of renunciation. And in so doing He won the victory that opened up citizenship in His Kingdom to all who believe.

That is what we are living for, and that is what we are waiting for. We have eternal life in the heavenly kingdom waiting for us after death. Why would we put all our chips on this blip on the timeline of eternity? You are like the flower that blossoms today but scorches in the sun – gone before you know it (Isaiah 40:6). This life is too short to deserve all of your effort and affection.

We should be filled with pity for the world around us. It is true that 1 John 2:15 tells us not love "the world or the things in the world," as a corrupt system of wickedness. But we are to love the world like Jesus did, as a place filled with people destined for eternity in Hell (John 3:16). This is why we can even endure suffering at their hands, because as

Jesus said, "they know not what they do" (Luke 23:34). Don't let the rocks cry out, Christian. Pray for the citizens of this world's kingdom. Weep for them. Love them enough to tell them the truth. Let your light shine before men with all the brilliance of the glory of God.

And if all of this sounds foreign to you, if the Kingdom of God is as unfamiliar to you as a kingdom on the Moon, let me say that today can be your day of transformation. This is the hard truth, but you must hear it:

You have offended God by your sins, and you are destined to suffer His wrath forever in Hell. Death will provide no release for you; only eternal torment awaits you beyond the grave. But there is Good News! The reason Jesus came down to Jerusalem in the first place was so that He might die on the cross. He took the penalty for your sin in His body on the cross so that I could make this offer to you. Everyone who calls out to God and asks for His forgiveness will receive it. If you repent of your sins, believe that Jesus died and rose again and commit your life to Him as the Son of God – your new King – then your destiny will change forever. You will gain a new citizenship in a Kingdom yet to come. There is nothing you must do to earn it. It is the free gift of God. Why live your life for the fleeting pleasures of this world, when there is an eternal Kingdom waiting for you on the other side?

"Well hold on!" you might say, "Are you asking me to sign up for all this pressure and persecution you just talked about?" Yes I am. Why? Because the glories of the abundant life in Jesus Christ and the hope of eternity are so splendid that all the rest of it pales in comparison. To try and minimize it, or to go back to the way we were would be utter foolishness.

That is the message, Christians. That is a message worthy dying for. More than that, it is a message worth living for. Living loud and proud, as they say! Don't expect the love of the world, you are not one of them. "If you were of the world," Jesus said, "the world would love you as its own; but because you are not of the world, but I chose you out of the world, therefore the world hates you" (John 15:19). If you can accept that, the pressures of this world will hold no temptation for you. Never give in, never give up, and never, ever be silent!

3

Whose House?

The Cleansing of the Temple

INTRODUCTION

Jesus lived on the earth for 30 years before He began His ministry. His ministry lasted 3 years. At least three times a year He would have gone to the Temple to worship for the major feasts. That amounts to at least 99 visits to the Temple. Knowing Jesus, I'm sure it was more. During His life, Jesus made perhaps hundreds of visits to the Temple. And I am sure that every time He did, His anger was aroused.

The Temple had become not just a house of worship, as it was intended to be, but in some respects it looked more like a marketplace. The Court of the Gentiles – the outer court where anyone could worship – had become a thoroughfare, with people using the Temple as a shortcut. There, sacrifices were purchased with money, but the Temple only accepted the Hebrew shekel, so there were places to change coinage. And through these "services", the religious leaders ripped the people off and made themselves rich.

A man named Annas had been appointed High Priest by the Roman authorities. He bribed his way into the most holy office in the land. Annas himself was deposed by Rome, but he was able to have 5 sons, a son-in-law and a grandson succeed him. Why? Because the family of Annas the Sadducee controlled the Temple market. They made a profit on top of every coin exchange and on every approved sacrifice they sold.

The Pharisees were no lovers of Annas, but they said nothing. No one did. After all, the sacrifices needed to be procured, and the money changed. And it was only the Court of the Gentiles after all, why bother to make room for them? No one cared.

But Jesus cared.

For more than 30 years He had walked into the Temple past the scam artists at the gates and fumed. He knew it was a shameful thing to do in His Father's house. But His time had not yet come. So He was patient, waiting for His hour. Then, on Palm Sunday, the beginning of the final week of His life, Jesus' hour came. He rode into the city on Sunday, went to the Temple and then returned to Bethany. But on Monday, He came back.

"In the temple he found those who were selling oxen and sheep and pigeons, and the money-changers sitting there. And making a whip of cords, he drove them all out of the temple, with the sheep and oxen. And he poured out the coins of the money-changers and overturned their tables. And he told those who sold the pigeons, 'Take these things away; do not make my Father's house a house of trade.'" (John 2:14-16)

"And he would not allow anyone to carry anything through the temple. And he was teaching them and saying to them, 'Is it not written, 'My house shall be called a house of prayer for all the nations'? But you have made it a den of robbers.'" (Mark 11:16-17)

All four Gospels tell this story, when Jesus cleansed the Temple. It was not the people's house to abuse, it was His Father's house. It was His house. And when Jesus rode in as the King of the Jews, He finally did what He had no doubt longed to do all His life.

Let me ask you this: Whose house are you? Is your heart your own domain, or is Jesus Lord there? What about your church? Your family? I'll tell you now, it is rightfully His house. And Jesus is ready to clean house today.

THE TEMPLE OF THE HOLY SPIRIT

You mustn't think of the Temple like most movies depict it – all brown and dusty and deserted. The Bible speaks of intricately carved doors and colorful tapestries and skillful paintings and metalwork; most of it was overlaid with gold, and the white stones would have shone like a second sun atop the Temple Mount. For most worshipers, it was the most color and beauty they would ever see. Add to that the sounds of the musicians and singers, the smell of the barbecued sacrifices and incense. The Temple was a delight to the senses. It was to be the place where God would meet with His people.

The Temple had replaced the Tabernacle, or the Tent, which had been built by Moses in the wilderness. David desired to build God a permanent house in Jerusalem, but that privilege was given to his son, Solomon. When it was completed in 1 Kings 8, Solomon brought the Ark of the Covenant into the Most Holy Place and there was a great celebration with multitudinous sacrifices and songs. "And when the priests came out of the Holy Place, a cloud filled the house of the Lord, so that the priests could not stand to minister because of the cloud, for the glory of the Lord filled the house of the Lord" (1 Kings 8:10-11). It is astonishing to think that men would later have so little regard for such a place.

When Nebuchadnezzar sacked Jerusalem, the Temple was destroyed, blowing a crater in the hearts of the Hebrews. The books of Ezra and Nehemiah tell the story of those who returned to rebuild the city and the Temple. Despite their initial shoddy efforts, the Lord promised to bless that Temple even more than the first (Haggai 2:9). Later, Herod the Great would renovate the Second Temple and make it beautiful again. That was the Temple to which Jesus came.

And yet, for all that, Solomon recognized that there were limits to the Temple. "Will God indeed dwell on the earth?" he prayed, "Behold, heaven and the highest heaven cannot contain you; how much less this house that I have built!" (1 Kings 8:27). He knew that the building was just a building. It was the presence of God that made it special.

Stephen would take up this theme before the Sanhedrin in the book of Acts. They had accused him of blaspheming the Temple and threatening to destroy it. Stephen gave a long history all about God meeting with the heroes of the faith outside of the Promised Land and outside of the Temple. The point was, in agreement with Solomon, "The Most High does not dwell in houses made by hands" (Acts 7:48). Stephen was stoned for his courage, the first Christian martyr.

God was doing something new. In Acts 2, on Pentecost, the Holy Spirit fallen upon the Church. No longer was the presence of God confined to the Temple, but He had sent the same Spirit that filled the Holy of Holies into the hearts of His people. The veil of the Temple had been rent in two when Jesus died (Matthew 27:51) to symbolize that God was no longer keeping Himself in one place.

Paul would phrase it this way: "Do you not know that you are God's temple and that God's Spirit dwells in you?" (1 Corinthians 3:16). The very thing that made the Temple holy is true of you, Christian! You do not need to go to a special place or to a special person in order to meet with God. You've got Him in your heart, if indeed you have believed on Jesus Christ (Romans 8:9). That makes you a walking, talking Holy Place. Jesus died to make it so. Your sins have been covered and your soul has been cleansed. God has taken up residence within you.

And Paul knew, as I'm sure you must, that there is a weight of responsibility that comes with being a temple of God. "Do you not know that your body is a temple of the Holy Spirit within you, whom you have from God? You are not your own, for you were bought with a price. So glorify God in your body" (1 Corinthians 6:19-20). Just as it was incumbent upon the Israelites to keep the implements and instruments of the Temple sanctified and holy, so too you and I have a mandate to keep ourselves a fitting house for the Lord.

Therefore, when we read of Jesus cleansing the Temple, there is some very interesting application to be drawn. That was in a physical Temple, in God's Promised Land, but the example of Jesus tossing tables and driving out cattle is equally instructive for us. For our personal lives, our families, and most importantly our churches, we must learn the lesson that Jesus taught on that day: It's His house.

THE PURPOSE OF THE TEMPLE

If the Temple is God's house, then it is God who gets to determine its purpose. You are the temple of the Holy Spirit and therefore God gets to determine the purpose of your life. We are accustomed to customizing everything from our cell phones to our career paths and (unfortunately) even our religion. But "you are not your own" anymore. So we need to know the purpose of God's house. The answer to that question affects everything else.

Jesus proclaimed the purpose of the Temple when He cleansed it. In Mark 11 He said, "Is it not written, 'My house shall be called a house of prayer for all the nations'?". This is a reference to Isaiah 56, part of a longer passage that we'll examine in detail in just a moment. For now, let's look at the first part of that statement: "a house of prayer". In that Isaiah passage, the Lord identifies as His true people those who "keep justice, and do righteousness...who choose the things that please [Him] and hold fast [His] covenant". Those welcome in God's house are those who obey His Word and worship Him – most clearly demonstrated through prayer.

That's what the Temple was, a house of prayer. When Solomon dedicated the Temple, his primary request was that God would hear the prayers of His people in that place. He goes on and on, outlining the kinds of prayer that could be offered: for repentance, discernment, deliverance, affliction, sickness, war. He even extends his request to the Gentiles outside of the Land. The Temple was the place for prayers to be heard. God made His presence to be manifest so that people could come and encounter Him there.

As the living temple of the Holy Spirit, you have the same purpose. You can know God indirectly through other Christians and directly through His Word, but you will only know Him personally through prayer.

You, then, are to be a house of prayer. To pray is to speak to God, to have direct communion with Him. I cannot stress enough the priority of prayer in a Christian's life. Prayer is air! It is the mark of a true believer (Acts 9:11), it is our safeguard against sin and temptation (Mark 14:38), it is the means by which God has determined to release His power (James 5:15-16). The disciples did not ask Jesus how to preach or how to counsel or even how to lead worship. They asked Him, "Lord, teach us to pray" (Luke 11:1).

The purpose of prayer is to cultivate fellowship with God. Under this umbrella we could add the other spiritual disciplines: fasting, Scripture, worship and more – anything that draws you closer to Jesus. You were created to know God, not just intellectually, but through experience. At the Temple people could find God, but now God has found you. The life of a Christian is to be one of great and growing intimacy with the Trinity. Paul called that his greatest goal in life: "That I may know Him and the power of His resurrection" (Philippians 3:10). And the best part is that if we seek God, we will find Him! Proverbs 2:4-5 tells us, "If you seek it like silver and search for it as for hidden treasures, then you will understand the fear of the Lord and find the knowledge of God".

One of the Spirit's primary duties is to enable and empower prayer in your life. "Likewise the Spirit helps us in our weakness. For we do not know what to pray for as we ought, but the Spirit himself intercedes for us with groanings too deep for words" (Romans 8:26). The New Testament speaks often of praying in the Spirit (Ephesians 6:18, Jude 20). Because God's presence is within you, you are always where He can hear you. And the Holy Spirit, who is Triune with the Father and the Son, can bring your prayers to Heaven directly. He provokes you to pray, He gives you the power to pray, and He even polishes up your prayers so that they will be received. This is why Jesus could make such astonishing promises concerning prayer: "Until now you have asked nothing in my name. Ask, and you will receive, that your joy may be full" (John 16:24).

You were made to know God. To read His Word, to fellowship with His people, to sing His praises, to take steps of faith, and most of all to pray. The Bible tells us over and over again to pray, to keep praying, and then to keep right on praying (Luke 18:1, Ephesians 6:18, 1 Thessalonians 5:17). The early Church did not have a full New Testament yet, but they knew God. For they knew that it was His house, and His house is always to be a house of prayer.

THE CORRUPTION OF THE TEMPLE

But Jesus had to cleanse the Temple. As He turned the tables, He reminded them of the purpose of the Temple, and then accused them of corrupting that purpose: "You have made it a den of robbers...Do not make my Father's house a house of trade". Rather than a house of prayer, the Temple had become a house of trade and a den of thieves.

That accusation, "a den of robbers", was another reference to the Old Testament. Jeremiah was the son of a priest, sent to call out the wickedness of Temple worship in Jerusalem. He said in Jeremiah 7:9-11, "Will you steal, murder, commit adultery, swear falsely, make offerings to Baal, and go after other gods that you have not known, and then come and stand before me in this house, which is called by my name, and say, 'We are delivered!' – only to go on doing all these abominations? Has this house, which is called by my name, become a den of robbers in your eyes?" In Jeremiah's day, the people would commit grievous sins and then come to God's house without the slightest blush of guilt. It was the same in Jesus' day.

They had clogged up the Outer Court, the Court of the Gentiles, with merchandise. They were changing money and selling sacrifices, and making a profit off the worship of God. People would carry burdens through the Temple as a shortcut for their commerce. Something had gone very wrong. Jesus echoed the words of Jeremiah, asking the Jews how they could stomach to worship in God's house when just behind that wall, filthy lucre was at work, and the Gentiles were being excluded.

This brings us back to His other allusion, that of Isaiah 56. The Temple was not just a house of prayer, but a house of prayer for "all the nations". That word for "nations" is *ethne* in Greek, and *goyim* in Hebrew. It could just as easily be translated "Gentiles". God had set up the Court of the Gentiles so that those who were not ethnic Israelites could still come and worship Him. Solomon specifically prayed for such people; those like Cornelius the centurion (Acts 10) or the eunuch from Ethiopia (Acts 8).

But instead, the Outer Court was being used to make money. It was more like a bazaar than a house of worship. Gentiles and eunuchs would never have been able to find a place to pray there, and the Jews didn't worry themselves about it. Something needed to change, and that's where Jesus comes in.

How does this apply to you and me as the Temple of the Holy Spirit? Most obviously, this should apply to our churches. Everyone should be welcome to worship at any church at any time. The Church is the living fulfillment of God's promises in Isaiah 56. Every outcast and foreigner should have a place in God's house. It's a shame that our churches are so balkanized. There are rich churches and poor churches, liberal churches and conservative churches, lively churches and quiet churches. Most Christians would never go so far as to kick someone out they didn't like, but there are other ways of making sure nobody from outside feels comfortable. And don't think for a minute that this only happens "downward". There are poor churches that would be upset if a rich man walked in – and vice versa! It's the same sin, in whatever direction it flows.

What about buying and selling in the Temple? This applies to our churches too. God's house is no place for commerce, and yet preaching and publishing and worship music have become big business. But let's look at your own life. How does commerce keep you from prayer? Your business, your job, your hobbies? It is all too common for us to neglect prayer and neglect church because of work, or because of our children's activities. We have business to take care of, so that's what fills up our time that would otherwise be spent in prayer. The temple of God, which is your body, is full of the hustle and bustle of moneymaking (or money-spending), but has been completely detached from its purpose, which is to know God.

Anything, whether inherently wicked or not, that keeps you from fellowship with God, from being a house of prayer – is sin. You might say, "Well it's my life." But it's not your life, for you have been "bought with a price".

It's not your house. It's His house.

THE CLEANSING OF THE TEMPLE

On Monday morning, Jesus strode into His Father's house, with all the Messianic authority of the Son of David. And John 2:15 adds a very significant detail: "Making a whip of cords, he drove them all out of the temple.

Jesus made a whip.

This is the Greek word *fragellion*, a derivative from the Latin *flagellum*. This was a scourge. It comes from the same root as when it says He was "scourged" (Matthew 27:26). We aren't given any details about what it looked like, but this thing was sufficient to send people running.

Every movie gets this wrong. Jesus did not bump over a little table while everyone watched. He had a whip! Maybe He was braiding it the night before, or maybe He worked on it in the Temple court itself. What do you think the disciples were thinking as they watched Him? But whatever the case, He showed up Monday ready to take care of business.

Picture it in your mind: Jesus stands up in the loud, crowded court and CRACK goes the whip!

"Alright!" He roars. "Everyone out!"

Perhaps they are slow to move at first. Maybe the Temple moneychangers scoff at Him and tell Him to move along. Then two strong carpenter arms reach under the heavy wooden table and flip it over. The sound of clinking coins echoes as they roll on the stone floor. The men are angry and turn to Jesus, but CRACK! they feel the sting of the whip across their backs and arms.

"How dare you defile my Father's house!"

Now a woman screams. People are turning and murmuring. Jesus turns over another table, and continues to swing the whip. A few try to stop Him, but the *flagellum* in His hand and the fire in His eyes sends them all running. Even the disciples stand back, shocked and astonished at what they're seeing from their Master.

Then Jesus goes to the stockades and turns the animals loose. Oxen and sheep begin to press as He lashes them forward. The oxen low and toss their heads, and a stampede begins in the Court of the Gentiles! People shove each other out of the way, making for the door. Jesus orders those selling the birds to get them out. It's a madhouse! People dodging heavy oxen, scooping down to pick up coins, cursing, shouting, and above it all the *CRACK* of Jesus' whip.

The stampede rumbles on, and Jesus – no one daring to approach Him now – stands alone and shouts at the top of His lungs, "It is written!" He rebukes the people with violent energy. Then He goes to the doors of the Temple and refuses to allow the merchants to finish their routes. "Get these things out of here! This isn't your shortcut!" It would not have been a quick process, it would have gone on for some time, until folks got the message.

At last, any lingering moneychanger is long gone. The Court is a mess, the tables are broken, sheep and goats wander around. The only ones remaining are Jesus of Nazareth, His hand still gripping that whip, His breath seething, and the Twelve, who have never seen Him like this. Then, "His disciples remembered that it was written, 'Zeal for your house will consume me'" (John 2:17).

Does it surprise you to think that Jesus made a whip? And don't think for a moment that He held it like a prop – Jesus used that thing. It chafes against our modern ideas of "gentle Jesus, meek and mild" doesn't it? It chafes against

71

our Christian ideas of violence and manhood. But there it is, in your Bible.

The Lord had spoken through Malachi saying, "Oh that there were one among you who would shut the doors, that you might not kindle fire on my altar in vain!" (Malachi 1:10). God wished some righteous soul would put a stop to the iniquity He saw in His Temple. So when God came in the flesh, that is exactly what He did. "I the Lord your God am a jealous God" (Exodus 20:5), the Lord said, "My glory I will not give to another" (Isaiah 48:11). When the house of God has been corrupted, this is how Jesus handles things.

It's how Jesus taught us to handle our own sin, too. "If your right eye causes you to sin," He said, "tear it out and throw it away. For it is better that you lose one of your members than that your whole body be thrown into hell" (Matthew 5:29). The purity of the temple of God requires radical repentance. We can't tiptoe around sin and have dozens of committee meetings deciding how to handle it. Jesus made a whip!

You were made to know God, and yet your heart has been corrupted by lesser things. You have hate in your heart, excluding those from fellowship whom God has accepted. You are bound by greed for gain, and have prioritized money over prayer. You take shortcuts, using the Church as a social club or a place for business connections. Shame on you! Shame on me, shame on all of us who have defiled the Father's house with our own nonsense.

There is no secret sauce to repentance. How do we eliminate sin? We cut out the infection. We amputate the limb. Whatever that looks like for you, you must do it. End that friendship. Delete that account. Quit that job. Cut up that credit card. Publicly apologize. I can't tell you specifically, but the Holy Spirit can, and He right now is putting His finger on the things that you must eliminate. The things you must drive out of your life with a whip, and then refuse to allow back inside with those same burdens.

"If you live according to the flesh you will die, but if by the Spirit you put to death the deeds of the body, you will live" (Romans 8:13). Paul said that; a man who knew a thing or two about renouncing the old life. Enough with this one-step-at-a-time nonsense. You know what must be done, it's time to do it. It's not enough to agree that it would be a good idea to deal with your sin, and get all emotional at church, you must do it! How many epiphanies do you need before you take the obvious course of action?

You are the temple of the Most High God. You are not your own – it's His house! Be zealous for His house (Psalm 69:9), as He was, and drive out the iniquity.

THE JOY OF THE TEMPLE

What happened afterwards? As might be expected, the Jews demanded to know how He dared do such a thing. (This probably happened later, after He had cooled down!) That's when He gave that prophecy of His resurrection: "Destroy this temple, and in three days I will raise it up" (John 2:19). A cryptic answer, because Jesus was not about to abase Himself to the demands of these corrupt schemers. For the rest of the week, the Pharisees and Sadducees and scribes and priests interrogated Him, trying to embarrass Him in front of everyone, of course to no avail. And they all determined that it was now time for Jesus to die (Mark 11:18). He had said and done so many things over 3 years, but it was when He messed with their money that they finally took action.

But there is more. After Jesus had cleared out the Court, people flocked to Him. "The blind and the lame came to him in the temple, and he healed them," and "children [were] crying out in the temple, 'Hosanna to the Son of David!'" (Matthew 21:14-15). The Temple finally achieved a semblance of what it was supposed to be. A place of healing, a place of praise, and a place where people might come to know the Lord.

Repentance can be rough. But when we see our sin clearly, there's nothing else we can do but deal with it. And

that's a painful process. You begin to see just how messed up you really are, and
how unable you are to handle yourself on your own. But if you allow that not to break you, but to drive you into the arms of your Savior, you will find a joy like no other. Jesus will heal your blindness and your lameness and put a song of praise in your mouth. Yes, He was angry at the sinners in the Temple, how could He not be? They were preventing people from coming to Him. But to those who did come, there was only love and grace. "A bruised reed he will not break, and a faintly burning wick he will not quench" (Isaiah 42:3). Jesus isn't looking to snuff you out, but to make things right and allow you to fulfill your purpose as His temple.

Nothing in life satisfies, does it? Haven't you had those moments where you get a bit of perspective? I find it's usually after a great accomplishment. There's the initial exuberance, but then when it calms down, you think – "Well, now what?" The thought of working every day until we die, or putting up with pain and heartache for another decade can be unbearable. What's the point of it all?

You feel this way because you are not living out the purpose for which you were created. Especially if you are a Christian. Once you have committed your life to Christ, you have made yourself permanently unable to be satisfied with anything else. To ignore the God who dwells within you is to be in constant unresolved conflict in your very soul. And it's never over anything good! The things that keep us from God are always lesser things: having more money, being more attractive, having more influence, enjoying more things. All of that is fleeting. But if we let the world tell us what is important and good, then we will be out of alignment with the Holy Spirit.

Jesus is a healer. Come to Him with your blindness: your inability to see things for what they are, the lies you've believed, the accusations you've accepted. Even the theories and philosophies you've swallowed that poison your love for Christ. Jesus will open your eyes! You'll see Him with a freshness you never thought you could recover. The things of God will seem bright and glorious to you in contrast to the shabby offerings of the Devil.

Come to Him with your lameness. What scars do you have? Where are you walking with a limp because of something that's happened to you? Jesus wants to heal that. Believe it or not, sometimes we can be so tied to our pain that the thought letting go is terrifying. We define ourselves by our bitterness or unforgiveness or depression or lack of trust for people. But Jesus can straighten all that out. And you'll be able to think on those things or love those people without the shooting pain that you're accustomed to. You'll be leaping and dancing before the Lord!

And He'll put a new song of praise in your mouth, because worship and prayer will no longer be a chore, but a delight. You'll understand why some in your church weep and shout and grin like fools during the opening songs. Simple truths that you learned way back in Vacation Bible School will flow from your lips with new profundity and new understanding. Once you clear the corruption out, the joys of being a temple of the Holy Spirit will overwhelm the loss of what you've left behind.

CONCLUSION

When I played basketball in middle school, we used to have a chant to get us hyped up for the game. The team captain, Brian, would shout, "Whose house?" and we'd all answer, "Our house!" Faster and faster we'd go, claiming that spot as our territory. It was especially fun at away games because of course it wasn't our house! But the defiance made it even better.

If Jesus had been in the Temple and asked, "Whose house?" the only right answer could have been, "Your house". When we walk into church, the pastor might ask, "Whose house?" and every finger should point upward – "His house". You look in the mirror every morning, and if you listen, you can hear the Holy Spirit whisper to you,

"Whose house?" You ought to bow your head and answer humbly, "Your house".

It's His house! You are the temple of the Holy Spirit of Christ. You have no claim to yourself, because Jesus bought you with His blood.

The path to obedience involves making room. Every part of you must be in submission to Him. That is the shortest path to peace and joy. So make room in every room. Every house has "that" room, or "that" closet, or "that" drawer that's filled to bursting with junk. Jesus wants to open up that closet and clear it out and sanctify it into a house of prayer. This can be a hard process, but it must be done.

It's His house, after all.

4

Love Like This

The Last Supper

THE LAST SUPPER

"Now before the Feast of the Passover, when Jesus knew that his hour had come to depart out of this world to the Father, having loved his own who were in the world, he loved them to the end. During supper, when the devil had already put it into the heart of Judas Iscariot, Simon's son, to betray him, Jesus, knowing that the Father had given all things into his hands, and that he had come from God and was going back to God, rose from supper. He laid aside his outer garments, and taking a towel, tied it around his waist. Then he poured water into a basin and began to wash the disciples' feet and to wipe them with the towel that was wrapped around him." (John 13:1-5)

The Last Supper was Thursday night, the end of quite a week. On Sunday, Jesus had ridden into Jerusalem on a donkey, to wild acclaim from the crowds. On Monday, He had gone into the Temple and driven out the money changers with a whip. On Tuesday He had wrangled with the Pharisees and Sadducees in the Temple courts and gotten the better of them in every debate. On Wednesday, He had delivered the Olivet Discourse to His disciples, prophesying the destruction of Jerusalem and the end of the world. And the Gospels are full of other marvelous things that took place during this Holy Week, all of which are worth your time and devotion.

Now it is Thursday. Jesus' disciples have prepared the Upper Room for the Passover feast. The meal was to be held at twilight, so sometime in the afternoon Peter and John would have gone to sacrifice a lamb in the Temple. They would have prepared unleavened bread and wine and bitter herbs for the meal. Meanwhile, Jesus was probably extricating Himself from the crowds. No doubt He was stopped along the way by countless enthusiastic supporters, treating Him like a celebrity or a revolutionary. However it may have gone, they arrived at the place around late afternoon, and tramped up the stairs into a scene that would be immortalized forever in Holy Scripture.

I'm sure the young men who followed Jesus were

boisterous and excited as they sat down. Whether Peter and John were waiting for them, or the other way around, they would have excitedly discussed all that happened; sharing stories from the day, planning for the future, trying to one-up one another as they always did. And as they gabbed, they took off their sandals at the door – and no one washed anyone else's feet.

This was part of the culture of the day. Because everyone wore sandals, and the roads were not paved, a person's feet would become filthy. If you have ever been to a third-world country and seen the livestock and other feral animals prowling the streets, you have an idea of what this was like. Add to this the fact that people in the orient would recline at table next to each other, and the need for foot washing becomes obvious. As part of the code of hospitality, the host of a meal was to provide a means for the feet to be washed. Typically, this was a servant, the lowest of the low, the ultimate unskilled position. If there was no servant, then the children would do it, according to age. If the host had no children, his wife would do it, and if he was unmarried, the host himself would wash the feet of his guests. To not offer to wash the feet of a guest was very rude (Luke 7:44). So Jesus and the disciples were ready to eat their Passover meal. And no one's feet had been washed.

It does not say if the disciples were arguing about this, but I can imagine it was starting to become tense in the room as time went on and no one raised a hand to volunteer. The disciples were always jockeying for position. Several times in the Gospels we see them arguing over which one of them was the greatest. In fact, Luke 22:24 tells us that they would argue over that exact thing during this Last Supper. So for one of them to stoop down and wash the others' feet would be to take himself out of the running for "the greatest" by admitting that he was the least of them all.

But Jesus had told them in Matthew 23:11, "The greatest among you shall be your servant." And on this night, despite the horrific preoccupations running through His mind, He gave them the greatest illustration of servant leadership the world had ever seen. Jesus "laid aside his outer garments" (we might say He "rolled up His sleeves") and quietly, without announcing Himself, poured water into a basin and began to wash their feet.

I'll bet that when they noticed what He was doing, this rowdy crew fell silent. No doubt they were shamed by the humility of their Teacher, who did not shrink from performing a task the rest of them had been too proud to do. It may not have been clear who was the lowest on the ladder, but it was obvious who was on the top. And He was the one washing their feet.

In verse 14, Jesus said, "If I then, your Lord and Teacher, have washed your feet, you also ought to wash one another's feet." The Bible is full of descriptions of humility and love, but Jesus showed us what love really looks like, what humility really looks like. It is this practical, sacrificial love that we are to imitate towards one another.

This passage tells us four things that were on Jesus' mind before He washed the disciples' feet. We know what we are to do, we are to "wash each others' feet". That is, to love each other practically and humbly. These thoughts of Jesus tell us why and how. By learning to think like Jesus thought, we will learn to act like Jesus acted and to love like He loved.

HE WAS GOING TO THE CROSS

Number one, Jesus knew He was going to the cross. It says, "Jesus knew that his hour had come to depart out of this world to the Father". The time had finally come for Him. Jesus was the Son of God, but He was also the Son of Man. He did not face His fate with cold, stoic logic. He felt the fear deep in His bones. In a few hours He would be in the Garden of Gethsemane, "in agony," as Luke said, "his sweat...like great drops of blood falling down to the ground" (Luke 22:44).

The Roman cross was a torturous way to die. The nails in the wrists and ankles provided the only support to the battered body hanging there. The eventual death was from asphyxiation, although Jesus Christ would die sooner, from blood loss and trauma after the scourging He endured. In the previous chapter He said, "Now is my soul troubled. And what shall I say? 'Father, save me from this hour'? But for this purpose I have come to his hour" (John 12:27). But despite the agony of mind He was enduring now, and the physical agony He would endure in a few short hours, He was not about to turn aside from His mission.

Jesus was born that He might die as a sacrifice upon that cross. This was an event in time (ca. 30 A.D.), but it was God's plan from the very beginning. Paul says in Ephesians 1:7-10, "In him," that is, Jesus, "we have redemption through his blood, the forgiveness of our trespasses, according to the riches of his grace, which he lavished upon us, in all wisdom and insight making known to us the mystery of his will, according to his purpose, which he set forth in Christ as a plan for the fullness of time, to unite all things in him, things in heaven and things on earth".

In eternity past, before the first act of Creation, the Holy Trinity purposed to redeem those made in His image. God would not allow the deceit of Satan to ruin the world He had made, nor to steal away the children He had fashioned with His own hands. But in order to effect their redemption, a man without sin must die as a sacrifice for all of humanity. There was no such man. That is why the Son of God, the Word, the *Logos* of God, would have to become a man. Only as a man could He die for men, but only as God could He die for all men.

Philippians 2 tells us that Christ, "though he was in the form of God, did not count equality with God a thing to be grasped," or held onto tightly, "but emptied himself, by taking the form of a servant, being born in the likeness of men" (Philippians 2:6-7). The Holy Spirit overshadowed the Virgin Mary in the greatest miracle the world will ever know: God became a Man. He lived as we did and experienced all the joys and sorrows of life on earth. While He had full access to holy omnipotence and the command of legions of angels, He did not avail Himself of these divine privileges, but lived in abject humility, as we do. In fact, that passage continues, "he humbled himself by becoming obedient to the point of death, even death on a cross" (Philippians 2:8). Jesus was born to die.

And He knew it. As He said in John 12:27, "For this purpose I have come to this hour". This was always the final destination. No matter how large the crowds grew, and no matter how sweet life was to Him, He knew that at the end of it waited a cross. He knew it here at the Last Supper. So few things remained between Him and that suffering. When He came to the Upper Room, it was the first thing on His mind. He "knew that his hour had come to depart out of this world to the Father," and that road led first through Calvary.

Yet despite the gravity of the moment, despite the fear

that would set Him to shaking later, and despite the fact that He was the very Son of God in human flesh, He knelt down and began to wash His disciples' feet. That is the same love that sent Him to the cross. This is sacrificial love. If He was willing to lay down His life for these men, how could He fail to show them common hospitality?

The cross was Jesus' supreme motivation, the reason for His very life. It is to be the supreme motivation of our lives as well. Why should we show sacrificial love for our brothers and sisters? Because Jesus Christ showed sacrificial love to us on the cross.

A Christian is willing to sacrifice in order to love someone else. Love that gives up nothing is not real love. We may talk of love and sing of love and think pious thoughts about love, but if we are unwilling to make the sacrifice in the moment, then we have not learned what love really means. John wrote, "By this we know love, that he laid down his life for us, and we ought to lay down our lives for the brothers. But if anyone has the world's goods and sees his brother in need, yet closes his heart against him, how does God's love abide in him? Little children, let us not love in word or talk but in deed and truth" (1 John 3:16-18).

Love under the cross is not afraid to sacrifice time. Jesus had less than 24 hours to live, and yet he took one of them to wash the feet of His Twelve disciples. We are so stingy with our time. It seems like we only ever work or worship or talk on the phone so that we can hang up and get back to serving ourselves. Don't mimic the attitude of the world that even resents the time they give to their own children. Take the time to listen to one another, don't rush out of conversation. Take the time to enjoy each other's company, don't count the minutes. And take the time to notice when someone's feet might need washing; that is, when they are in need of your sacrificial love.

Love under the cross is not afraid to sacrifice effort. Jesus had to get down on His knees and perform a task that most slaves did not even have to do. We love the idea of sacrificial love – until someone needs help moving. Or until they need us to bring them a can of gasoline on the freeway. And even if we do step out to help, we grumble and complain the whole way. Help one another, and do a great job. Babysit children, help change the tire, cover the lawncare while they are sick. The world sees it as rude to presume upon someone's help, but in the Church we have a default attitude of sacrificial love.

And love under the cross is not afraid to sacrifice resources. This is where most of us draw the line. I'll help, I'll listen, I might even pray for you, but asking for money is entirely inappropriate. Did you not hear what John said a moment ago? If you have the means to help somebody and withhold it, how can you claim to be a child of the cross? What did Jesus withhold from us? Be generous with your money, and give freely. If you have no money to give, what do you have? Do you have skills or tools or education? Tabitha made clothes for the widows in Acts 9, and the church grieved for her so much, God granted her a resurrection! Sacrificial love actively seeks out opportunities to wash the feet of the brethren in the Church, because we have the example of Jesus on the cross..

Paul told the Corinthians, "For I decided to know nothing among you except Jesus Christ and him crucified" (1 Corinthians 2:2). That's why he could travel around the Mediterranean Sea and endure prison, beatings and slander in every city. The cross was enough of a motivation for him. When everything else is stripped away, it is still true that Jesus died for us. That should compel our behavior towards one another. Jesus knew He was going to the cross, and He still washed the feet of the disciples.

HE LOVED HIS DISCIPLES

The second thing we see is that Jesus knew He loved His disciples. "Having loved his own who were in the world, he loved them to the end". Maybe Jesus stood back from the bustle of the room for a minute and took a long look at each disciple in turn, knowing that this was the end of a long road that would not resume until He came again in His Kingdom. He loved His disciples not just with the sacrificial love of the cross, but with the sincere love of a friend and brother. "Greater love has no one than this," He would tell them later that night, "that someone lay down his life for his friends. You are my friends if you do what I command you. No longer do I call you servants, for the servant does not know what his master is doing; but I have called you friends, for all that I have heard from my Father I have made known to you" (John 15:13-15).

There was a story behind the inclusion of each one of these Twelve. Some of them are known to us through the Gospels. Andrew was a disciple of John the Baptist until John identified Jesus as the Lamb of God. He seems to have been the entry point for many of the future apostles. James and John were his fellow fishermen, as was his brother Simon Peter. Peter of course was chosen by Jesus when He gave them that miraculous catch of fish on the Sea of Galilee. Philip was from their hometown, and if Nathanael was Bartholomew, as some have speculated, so was he. Matthew was a tax collector, probably the one who took taxes from the fishing boats of these other disciples. He left his tax table and brought all of his wealthy, sinful friends to meet Jesus at his house. The other Simon was a Zealot, a revolutionary of radical political ideals. I wonder what his story was like? I wonder about Thomas and Thaddeus and not least of all Judas Iscariot.

Luke tells us 6:12-13, "In these days he went out to the

mountain to pray, and all night he continued in prayer to God. And when day came, he called his disciples and chose from them twelve, whom he named apostles". Jesus, after a nightlong vigil in prayer, handpicked these men out of the multitudes who followed Him. These Twelve were first called, according to Mark 3:14, "that they might be with him". They were to be His constant companions for three years, more than His mother, His brothers or anyone else.

Together these men had spent countless days walking and nights out in the open. They had been through all the land of Israel and even up into the Decapolis together. Before their very eyes Jesus had taught His parables, healed the sick, raised the dead, walked on water and multiplied the loaves and the fishes. More than that, every one of these men would have had personal stories of their interaction with Jesus. The little details that wouldn't mean anything to anybody else, but in the years to come would be more precious than silver. Jesus had those moments, too. He knew their personalities and idiosyncrasies, their backgrounds, their failures, their successes, their fears and their dreams. And He loved them.

So He decided to wash their feet. This was not just another parable to illustrate a point, He wanted to show them how much He loved them. They had done so much for Him that He wanted a chance to serve His friends. I wonder if His hands shook as He went from person to person, or if each one got a personal, last word from the Lord. We'll never know. But it certainly made an impression on them.

Of course, when He got to Peter, there was a hiccup. Peter, out of His sincere respect for Jesus (and perhaps too out of a soulish desire to show off!) refused to let Jesus wash his feet. He knew how the culture worked, and by allowing Jesus to wash his feet, he would be acknowledging that he was higher than his Lord. I love Jesus' wonderful patience with Peter. He knew that each one of His disciples was unique, and needed to be loved in their own way. He knew that Peter was stouthearted and stubborn, qualities that would serve the Church well once the Spirit had come upon him. No one else needed an explanation, but Peter did, and so Christ gave it to him. He loved Peter's zeal; He did not hold it against him.

Paul wrote in Romans 12:9, "Let love be genuine". That word for "genuine" is *anupokritos* in Greek, literally "without hypocrisy". He goes on in the next verse to say, "Love one another with brotherly affection. Outdo one another in showing honor". Jesus not only taught us sacrificial love, He taught us sincere love. Just as His love for the disciples moved Him to wash their feet, our sincere love for one another ought to move us to wash one another's feet.

Hypocritical love is about the greatest insult one person could offer another. Hypocritical love will roll its eyes the second the person has turned to go. Hypocritical love will keep checking their phone while a brother in Christ is pouring out his heart. Hypocritical love will write sweet things in the birthday card but then write something sarcastic and nasty in the private chat. This is not the kind of love we are supposed to have.

Some people love humanity in a broad sense. Many activists claim to have great love for humanity, but in person they seem to be the most angry, violent people. Why is that? I thought they loved people? That is just it – they love "people". They love people in an abstract way. They do not love the world as a collection of individuals, but as a mass. Sometimes they insist that the world must be improved by force, because the masses are too much like sheep to be good for anything but slaughter. Jesus sees us as sheep too, but He is a Good Shepherd who leaves the ninety-nine to care for the one. These other groups believe that as long as they do what is best for the people, it does not matter if they love them or not. True love is in the doing, right?

Well, it is true that love is a verb. Jesus demonstrated that by dying on the cross and by washing their feet. Paul said "Outdo one another in showing honor". But all of that is built upon genuine, non-hypocritical love. Jesus is different from other moral teachers because He requires of us the proper motivations, not just the proper actions. In the

Old King James, they translated literally from the Greek and called it "bowels" of mercy. We use the heart as the organ that represents the emotion of love, but they used the bowels. We might call it love on a gut level. You are not just called to do nice things for people, but to have actual affection for the people of God. Sincere love does not fake it, but trains the heart how to feel.

And let's be honest, some people are harder to love than others! Sometimes, people are more like Peter, who are suspicious and selfish when you try to show love to them. It would be so much easier if we could just dismiss these people and write them off, but Jesus has not given us that option. Have you ever been a part of a group that slowly gives someone the cold shoulder, hoping they'll go away? Some churches are like the Hunger Games, where the circle gets smaller and smaller until there's no one left. But if you persist in showing love to someone like Simon Peter, you will find that the most exhausting people can be the most loyal, affectionate friends you will ever make. It is worth putting forth the effort to love people, even the difficult ones.

If you want to train yourself to love sincerely, put in the time. Most people put up some kind of front when they meet someone. Even people who seem fun and outgoing often feel pressured to be funny and happy all the time. If you can be the one to stick with them once that façade slips, they will love you for it. So purpose to have conversations that go a little deeper than the surface each time. Say hello at church, invite them to a group function. Take the time to see who they really are, and love them how they need to be loved.

And take it to the Lord. God loves everyone sincerely – even you! God sees everything that is both lovable and unlovable about you and everyone else. He can show you what is worth loving in a person. Then God can use you to draw that potential out of them. We become a sanctifying presence for one another. If you just can't stand somebody, take it to the Lord in prayer. It's really hard to hate somebody after you've spent 100 hours in prayer for them.

Jesus knew He loved His disciples, and so He washed their feet. It is much easier to do something nice for somebody than to actually care for them, but the Lord requires that we do both. So if you have a hard time loving people for their own sake, do it for His. "Having purified your souls by your obedience to the truth for a sincere brotherly love, love one another earnestly from a pure heart" (1 Peter 1:22).

HE WAS GOING TO BE BETRAYED

Number three, Jesus knew He was going to be betrayed. "The devil had already put it into the heart of Judas Iscariot,

Simon's son, to betray him." When Judas realized that Jesus was serious about this "not-of-this-world" stuff, he went straight to the high priests to betray Him. Even during the Last Supper, there was a detachment of soldiers standing by to take Jesus into custody when Judas gave the signal. And Jesus knew. It says in verse 21: "After saying these things, Jesus was troubled in his spirit, and testified, 'Truly, truly, I say to you, one of you will betray me.'"

In verse 18 He referred to Psalm 41:9, "Even my close friend in whom I trusted, who ate my bread, has lifted his heel against me". It had been foretold that the Messiah would be betrayed to His death (Zechariah 11). "But woe," Jesus said in Mark 14:21, "to that man by whom the Son of Man is betrayed! It would have been better for that man if he had not been born." It had been prophesied, but Judas was not compelled. Or excused. He would sell Jesus out of his own accord, identifying Him to the soldiers with a kiss.

Jesus knew that. He knew that Judas was going to betray Him. But He washed his feet, too. Do you think He choked back tears as He remembered when Judas Iscariot first came to Him? Do you think He was surprised when His Father revealed to Him who the traitor was? There He is, in a supreme act of love and humility, washing the feet of His betrayer. It was exactly that kind of selfless love that Judas could not understand.

Just as Jesus knew He would be betrayed, we must

know that when we try to love other people, we will get burned along the way. But the kind of love that would wash the feet of a brother is a selfless love. If we were only in this for what we could get out of it, we would snatch back our love the second we knew someone was plotting against us. Don't love people for your own sake! That's not love, that's slavery. We must love people for their own sake, selflessly. Love is doing what is best for someone else, and "I" does not factor into the equation.

I have been betrayed before, although certainly not on the level that Jesus experienced. I have had people that I loved and served alongside for years work behind the scenes to stab me in the back. I am not a crier. In those instances I did not weep, but I grew angry. In one case, when I confronted the man and he still maintained that fake attitude, lying to my face, all I wanted to do was to swear him forever. "Go away, and who cares if I ever see you again!" Ah, but Jesus washed the feet of His betrayer, as Judas lied to his face by his very presence in that room.

If you are going to love people, you are going to be betrayed. There will be people who laugh with you, then spread rumors and lies behind your back. You will make a sacrificial gesture to watch them squander it. There will be times where someone weeps on your shoulder only to tell stories about how you never cared about them. You will pour your life and heart into people, take their midnight phone calls, walk with them through every crisis, defend their honor to people who try to warn you, and then they will break off the friendship without so much as a word. Don't wonder "if", know for a certainty that this will happen, and it will happen to you.

When David was king, his son Absalom secretly plotted against him and staged a coup, driving him out of Jerusalem in shame. David's wise counselor, Ahithophel conspired with Absalom to drive him out, and David's heart was broken. He wrote in Psalm 55:12-14, "For it is not an enemy who taunts me – then I could bear it; it is not an adversary who deals insolently with me – then I could hide from him. But it is you, a man, my equal, my companion, my familiar friend. We used to take sweet counsel together; within God's house we walked in the throng". Nothing hurts more than the betrayal of a brother or sister in Christ. The man who creeps in and splits the church to start his own. The woman who comes in for counseling then sues the church for sexual abuse when no such thing has happened. The co-laborer who publishes an article about the ineptitude of your ministry. It hurts, and it hurts worse than any outside persecution.

But this is what we are called to do. Jesus set the example to wash the feet even of our betrayers, or potential betrayers. We are not permitted to harden our hearts towards the people of God. We are to endure suffering even at the hands of the Church, and to trust God to sort out the harvest in the end. Even Jesus with His betrayer would say no more than, "What you are going to do, do quickly" (John 13:27).

Besides, who knows if the love you show in the midst of a betrayal might not turn a person's heart? Perhaps your readiness to forgive will melt the heart of stone and gain you an ally rather than an enemy. "Love bears all things, believes all things, hopes all things, endures all things" (1 Corinthians 13:7). Love is willing to believe that the traitor can be redeemed and hope that the prodigal will return, even when everyone else has given him up as hopeless.

Jesus knew He was going to be betrayed, and yet He washed the feet of His disciples anyway. Real love is selfless. Jesus saw the possibility – the certainty – of being hurt as worth the risk, and so should we.

HE HAD ALL AUTHORITY

Fourth and finally, Jesus knew He had all authority as the Son of God. He came to Supper that night, as it says in verse 3, "knowing that the Father had given all things into his hands, and that he had come from God and was going back to God". He emphasized this to His disciples as well in verse 13, "You call me Teacher and Lord, and you are right, for so I am". And yet, with all of that authority, the authority to call for "twelve legions of angels" (Matthew 26:53), He knelt down and washed their feet.

The events of that night were entirely in Jesus' hands. As He said in John 10:18, "No one takes [my life] from me, but I lay it down of my own accord. I have authority to lay it down, and I have authority to take it up again. This charge I have received from my Father". He did not have to go the cross, or stand trial in a kangaroo court, or be scourged. He was the Son of God, and He was and remains obligated to do nothing. Yet in the Garden of Gethsemane, He said to His Father, "Not my will, but yours, be done" (Luke 22:42).

That act of submission was the final confirmation that He would go to the cross, and He did. By submitting to His Father's will, He was humbled to lowest possible point, but now God has exalted Him to His right hand (Philippians 2:9). And someday Christ will return to take ownership of the Kingdom that is rightfully His, and He will reign for 1,000 years. "Then comes the end," according to 1 Corinthians 15:24, "when he delivers the kingdom to God the Father after destroying every rule and every authority and power."

Jesus chose to exercise His authority (His rights, you might say) in submission to the Father. He did not use His authority to make demands of the Twelve, but to demonstrate what godly authority looks like. He had taught them in Mark 10:42-45, "You know that those who are considered rulers of the Gentiles lord it over them, and their great ones exercise authority over them. But it shall not be so among you. But whoever would be great among you must be your servant, and whoever would be first among you must be slave of all. For even the Son of Man came not to be served but to serve and to give his life as a ransom for many". He had taught them this, and now He was showing them. He showed them what servant leadership looks like. Through this act He taught us that the key to godly authority is not dominance, but love and submission. By washing their feet, Jesus had, in a sense, submitted to His own disciples. To submit means to stand aside for somebody. He deferred His own rights to meet their needs. That is godly submission.

Christ's love is submissive, and yours should be, too. This means, first of all, that you recognize Christ's authority over you and do as He says, regardless of how it makes you feel. Jesus Christ has all authority, and He has told you to love to love your neighbor. "If I then," He said in verses 14-16, "your Lord and Teacher, have washed your feet, you also ought to wash one another's feet. For I have given you an example, that you also should do just as I have done to you. Truly, truly, I say to you, a servant is not greater than his maser, nor is a messenger greater than the one who sent him". Jesus has commanded you to love, and He outranks you. You have no right to withhold love from anybody.

That makes it pretty simple. You don't have to have a meeting with yourself to decide whether or not you want to love somebody. That decision has been made for you by the one who has all authority. He even said to "Love your enemies, do good to those who hate you, bless those who curse you, pray for those who abuse you" (Luke 6:28). It's a settled conclusion.

And He showed us too, that even if we do have authority over someone else, that does not excuse us from showing the kind of love that would wash another's feet. We are really big on rights in this country. We demand our rights, we march for our rights, we fight and die for our rights. But in the Church of Jesus Christ, it is all about dying to ourselves. The pyramid is inverted; those with the most authority are to be those who best exemplify submissive, servant leadership. That is why in the Church you should think nothing of seeing the millionaire scrub toilets while the professional janitor preaches. We don't insist on our own way, here. It is our joy to defer to one another.

Paul had to write to the Corinthians to correct a problem that might sound familiar to us. The Corinthians were a litigious people, always taking each other to court in order to get their "full rights", and this had bled over into the Church. In 1 Corinthians 6, Paul is flabbergasted that these people would be so obstinate as to need a heathen judge to settle their differences. "Brother goes to law against brother," he wrote in verses 6 and 7, "and that before unbelievers? To have lawsuits at all with one another is already a defeat for you. Why not rather suffer wrong? Why not rather be defrauded?" Did you catch that? "Why not rather be defrauded?" Submissive love does not insist on its own way. When we do that, the name of Christ is put to public shame.

Ephesians 5:21 says that we should always be "submitting to one another out of reverence for Christ". This does not eliminate the organization and hierarchy in the Church, the family, or the state. But it tells us how we are to act within those structures. If every one of us was willing to defer to the other, if we were to be truly seeking to "outdo one another in showing honor", there would be no power struggles or conflicts of any kind, for that matter. Godly authority is submissive. The Holy Trinity is three persons in harmonious hierarchy, in loving submission to one another. That is the very nature of God, and it is to be the very nature of God's people.

We do not respect rank and authority when it comes to love. James, the brother of Jesus, rebuked the churches for providing special seating and honor for dignified guests. He said in James 2:9, "If you show partiality, you are committing sin and are convicted by the law as transgressors". We don't operate like the world does. We live out submissive love, keeping in mind that Christ is the one with all authority, not us. And even He in His universal authority chose to humble Himself and serve in His final hours.

Jesus knew He had all authority as the Son of God. And yet He washed their feet. He went to the cross. And He taught us to do the same.

CONCLUSION

Those were the four things on Jesus' mind during the Last Supper: (1) He knew He was going to the cross, (2) He knew He loved His disciples, (3) He knew He was going to be betrayed, and (4) He knew He had all authority as the Son of God. He taught us that love is sacrificial, love is sincere, love is selfless, and love is submissive. And He demonstrated this in one powerful gesture by taking the lowest place and washing the feet of the disciples.

"Beloved, let us love one another, for love is from God, and whoever loves has been born of God and knows God. Anyone who does not love does not know God, because God is love" (1 John 4:7-8). Christ's example is difficult to follow, but when we consider what He did for us, loving the difficult, the traitor, the one beneath us – it all becomes so simple.

Jesus overcame the world, not with a sword, not with an army, not even with an idea. He overcame the darkness of the world through love. Ladies and gentlemen, this is how we will overcome. Love! Love like this. Love that Jesus demonstrated not only at the Last Supper, but in His last hours as He went to the cross for your sake and mine. We all want to see the world changed, we all want to see things turned around. It starts with God's people determining that we are actually going to do what He said, to live like He lived. Love one another with practical, sacrificial love, and you will shine the light of the Gospel that can never be overcome.

5

Blood Cries Out for Blood

The Crucifixion

INTRODUCTION

Jesus of Nazareth spent three years as a traveling rabbi and healer. He healed the sick, the leper and the lame, He opened the eyes of the blind, and on at least three occasions He raised the dead. He preached a message of repentance and love and obedience to God, and He attracted a large following. Then, after Passover, He was betrayed by one of His Twelve disciples to the religious rulers, who arrested Him in the secrecy of night. He was put on three separate trials, none of which could find a charge for which they could convict Him. But because of the violence of the mob that had grown outside of the governor's palace, Jesus was beaten, scourged and mocked by the Roman soldiers. They cried out for His death, and He carried His own cross to the top of Mount Calvary, where they crucified Him by nailing His hands and His feet to the beams and raising Him up above the crowds to suffocate in agony. In that humiliation and torment, Jesus Christ gave up His Spirit to God His Father and died.

This is a gruesome picture to consider, made all the worse by the fact that Jesus did not deserve any of this. He broke no law, He was entirely without sin, and yet they crucified Him anyway. Why? Why did Jesus die on the cross? The immediate cause, of course, was the jealousy of the Jewish leaders and the vicious crowd that supported them. But it goes deeper than that. Moments before His arrest, Jesus said in Matthew 26:56, "All this has taken place that the Scriptures of the prophets might be fulfilled". Jesus was the Son of God, and His death had been foretold long ago by the prophets. So then our question becomes: Why did God send His Son Jesus to die on the cross?

"But you have come to Mount Zion and to the city of the living God, the heavenly Jerusalem, and to innumerable angels in festal gathering, and to the assembly of the firstborn who are enrolled in heaven, and to God, the judge of all, and to the spirits of the righteous made perfect, and to Jesus, the mediator of a new covenant, and to the sprinkled blood that speaks a better word than the blood of Abel." (Hebrews 12:22-24)

It is this last verse on which I would like to focus our attention, Hebrews 12:24: "[We have come] to Jesus, the mediator of a new covenant, and to the sprinkled blood that speaks a better word than that of Abel". The author gives us two reasons here why the death of Jesus was necessary. First, Jesus came to mediate a better covenant. And secondly, it says that the blood of Christ speaks a better word than that of Abel.

This is of course a reference to Cain and Abel, the ancient story from the book of Genesis. To fully understand what this means, we will turn to that passage and take a closer look.

THE BLOOD OF ABEL

Cain and Abel were the two sons of Adam and Eve, born after they were driven from the Garden of Eden. When they brought sacrifices to the Lord, it says that the Lord received the offering of Abel, but rejected that of Cain. Despite a warning from God Himself, Cain lured his brother into the fields and killed him. God confronted Cain over what he had done and said in Genesis 4:10-11, "What have you done? The voice of your brother's blood is crying to me from the ground. And now you are cursed from the ground, which has opened its mouth to receive your brother's blood from your hand". And the Lord put a curse on Cain, that the ground would no longer produce food for him, and that he would be driven out from the society of other people.

The blood of Abel cried out to God from the ground. The horror of what Cain had done in committing the first murder shocked the whole world. The earth itself was reeling because it had been made to drink the blood of Man for the first time. The rebellion against God, we call it sin, that had begun in the Garden was now deep in the heart of Adam's children.

Why did Cain kill Abel? He first grew angry when he saw that God did not accept his offering, but accepted his brother's. But why would this lead to murder? John tells us in 1 John 3:12, "We should not be like Cain, who was of the evil one and murdered his brother. And why did he murder him? Because his own deeds were evil and his brother's righteous". Read that again: "Because his own deeds were evil and his brother's righteous".

Cain resented the light that Abel's life shed upon his own. Cain thought of himself as a decent man, but when he was compared to Abel before God, he came up short. This attitude is present in all of us. We come up with justifications for our actions and our attitudes. We tell ourselves that the way we are cannot be helped, or that the way we were raised has made our sins inescapable. But then we run up against someone who does not live the way we do. Someone who has perhaps experienced the same things we have, or worse, but has risen above it and not let themselves become vile. Maybe we even believe that it is impossible to be good only to then meet a good person. That can absolutely shatter the image a person has of themselves, and the results can be deadly. The apostle John put it this way, "This is the judgment: the light has come into the world, and people loved darkness rather than the light because their works were evil. For everyone who does wicked things hates the light and does not come to the light, lest his works should be exposed" (John 3:19-20).

Abel's righteousness exposed the evil in Cain's heart. And when Cain grew angry with Abel, God urged him to get control of himself because that attitude could have dire consequences. Cain did not listen, and that flaw in his heart became the defining act of his life. He tried to eliminate the object of comparison rather than make a change.

But as you know, the destruction of a standard does not change the rules. Abel was no longer there to expose Cain's faults by comparison, but Cain was still the same man. This is true at the highest level, because our standard for right and wrong is not one another, but God Himself. Abel was gone, but there was still God and His righteousness for Cain to be compared to. And after Cain murdered his brother, it was God's righteousness that stood in judgment of him.

What is the word, as the author of Hebrews would put it, that the blood of Abel spoke? It was justice. The ground itself cried out for justice. We love to talk about everyone getting what they deserve, but there are few things more terrifying than true, unmitigated fairness. The fair thing for Cain would have been for him to die as well. Blood cries out for blood.

But this would have been true regardless of whether Cain had killed Abel or not. God's standard is perfection, which none of us can meet. That wicked drive within each of us to shrink away from the light, or destroy the mirror that shows us who we really are – that drive is called sin. And it is internal. Cain did not murder his brother until they were in the fields, but he had a murderous heart within him long before that.

Each of us has that wickedness in our own hearts. It may lie dormant for a while, but given the proper trigger and the right opportunity, sin will rear up and reveal who we really are. We try to excuse our sin by comparing ourselves one to another, but that is unacceptable. The standard is God and His righteousness, and we all have missed the mark. And "the wages of sin is death," according to Romans 6:23. "The soul who sins shall die," says Ezekiel 18:4. There is no escaping it. The penalty for sin is eternal death in Hell;

eternal punishment for an eternal transgression. How many lives has your sin destroyed? How much joy have you stamped out? How many opportunities to show love have you scorned in exchange for your own selfishness? The blood of Abel cries out for justice.

What is there to be done? As Cain did, we cry out to God and ask if there is anything that might alleviate our punishment.

After the death of Abel, humanity spread across the globe, and wickedness proliferated. Telling the story of each individual murder would be too tedious and tragic to bother with. Then, out of His kindness, God chose a nation for Himself through which He would demonstrate the sinfulness of sin and provide an opportunity for atonement.

In the book of Exodus, God used Moses to bring His people out of slavery in the land of Egypt. He brought them through many dangers to Mount Sinai, where He made a Covenant with them. A Covenant is a solemn promise, a contract with obligations and penalties. The Lord promised to be their sovereign, blessing and protecting God if they would obey Him and be His people. On that first day, He gave them ten simple Commandments. You are familiar with these: "You shall have no other gods before me. You shall not make for yourself a carved image...You shall not take the name of the Lord your God in vain...Remember the Sabbath day, to keep it holy...Honor your father and mother...You shall not murder...You shall not commit adultery...You shall not steal...You shall not bear false witness...You shall not covet" (Exodus 20:3-17). This was the standard of righteousness to which God would hold these people.

But consider that list! Could you keep that list? Have you gone your whole life without lying or stealing or coveting or blaspheming? Even if you started over right now, could you? Of course not. And neither could they. That was the point. The Law existed to prove to the Israelites beyond a shadow of a doubt that they had missed the mark. They were sinners. It teaches us the same lesson. We resent the standard of righteousness, just like Cain did, because we know that we ourselves are not righteous.

So the Lord gave them more. He gave them an entire social structure and system of religious observance. He gave them a means by which they could come before Him and have their sins covered. But you will remember that "the wages of sin is death". Our sin cries out with the blood of Abel for justice. That is why the atonement for sins in the Temple had to be secured through blood.

Every time a sin was committed, the Israelite had to come to the Temple and offer a sacrifice of an animal with no blemishes. The Feasts and the Sabbaths were soaked in blood. Hebrews 9:22 tells us, "Indeed, under the law almost everything is purified with blood, and without the shedding of blood there is no forgiveness of sins". The blood of sin cries out for more blood, and so for hundreds of years the Jews worshiped God stained with the shed blood of innocent animals.

But something is not quite right, is it? I thought we were looking for justice. How can the death of an animal cover the sin of man or a woman? Imagine coming to the Temple and offering a lamb or a goat and then coming home to wash the blood from your hands. Then coming again the next year. And the next year. And the next year. Every time you sin you know you must go and atone for it. Slowly, you begin to realize: I can offer as many of these sacrifices as I want, but they are not solving the real problem. The problem is me. I don't just look bad because of the standard of the Law, the standard of the Law has shown me how rotten I really am. And if I am a sinner not just in the things I do, but in the very fiber of my being, how can I expect anything other than final condemnation when I stand before God?

This was exactly the point. God was teaching a lesson. A lesson that took centuries to learn, and even then, only by very few. Some of the prophets and poets of the Old Testament got it. "Samuel said," in 1 Samuel 15:22, "Has the Lord as great delight in burnt offerings and sacrifices as in obeying the voice of the Lord? Behold, to obey is better than sacrifice, and to listen than the fat of rams." David wrote in

Psalm 51, "For you will not delight in sacrifice, or I would give it; you will not be pleased with a burnt offering. The sacrifices of God are a broken spirit; a broken and contrite heart, O God, you will not despise". The writer to the Hebrews put it even more bluntly: "It is impossible for the blood of bulls and goats to take away sins" (Hebrews 10:4).

The Old Covenant, with all its glory, could only be a temporary fix. It served an important purpose, however: It held up a standard of righteousness in order to show us that the problem with us is on the inside, not the outside. And it demonstrated to the people the severity of sin by having them sacrifice animals in order to cover their own trespasses. The Law served to amplify the word spoken by Abel's blood: Justice! Blood for blood. And as the centuries ticked on by, the people of God began to realize that if there was to be any hope of forgiveness, it would not come through adherence to a standard. That would be impossible. The only hope was for God Himself to intervene.

THE BLOOD OF JESUS

So then let us return to Good Friday. Jerusalem is full of men and women come to worship at the Temple. The night before they had commemorated their deliverance out of Egypt by the sacrifice of a lamb and a meal of unleavened bread and bitter herbs. It is a sacred time of celebration and reflection. But there is a disturbance over at the governor's palace. A crowd has gathered to look into the courtyard, where the elders are arguing with the Roman governor on his judgment seat. Then, to an angry roar from the crowd, a man is brought forward. He can barely stand. His clothes have been stripped from him. His arms and legs are shackled together, and His back has been laid open by the cruel metal-studded scourge with which they have whipped Him. Around His head, branches from a thorn bush have been pressed together in mockery of a crown. "Behold your King!" says the governor, indicating the man next to him. But the people shout him down with manic voices, chanting, "Crucify! Crucify!" Pilate makes one final attempt to appeal to these Jews, but they shout him down once more. Finally, he collapses back onto his throne, calls for a basin of water, and washes his hands. With a wave of his arm, he leaves with his attendants, and Jesus of Nazareth is delivered over to the Praetorium for crucifixion.

Why was Pontius Pilate so reluctant to sentence Jesus to death? Because according to Matthew 27:18, "He knew that it was out of envy that they had delivered him up". Jesus died for the same reason Abel did. The religious rulers were jealous of Him But more than that, the land of Israel had had enough of Him. By His very life He shamed them. By His teachings He exposed their hypocrisy. Even by His

115

meekness in enduring the trial He blew apart the lies they had told themselves to justify their own behavior. The guilt was too much, and so the sons of darkness lied, bribed and betrayed that they might stamp out the Light of the world forever.

None of us can escape responsibility for what these men have done. You cannot blame the Jews, you cannot blame the Romans, you cannot blame a bygone generation. What was in their hearts is in your heart. How many times have you raged against beauty of God's Law because it stands in judgment of your own inadequacies? How virulently have you argued against the existence of God or of morality itself in order to escape the guilt that plagues you every time you turn out the lights? You were not there, but you have the same sin within your heart that shed the blood of Jesus. And blood cries out for blood.

But wait! Something is different. We read in Hebrews 12:24, "[We have come] to Jesus, the mediator of a new covenant, and to the sprinkled blood that speaks a better word than that of Abel". The blood of Jesus speaks a better word than the blood of Abel. What word is that? While Abel's blood, a symbol of all our wrongdoing, cries out for justice, the blood of Jesus cries out for mercy.

The death of Jesus was no accident. It was not some catastrophic miscarriage of justice that foiled God's eternal plan. As we said before, all of this was done to fulfill what had been spoken by the prophets. Isaiah said in his book, "He was pierced for our transgressions; he was crushed for our iniquities; upon him was the chastisement that brought us peace, and with his wounds we are healed. All we like sheep have gone astray; we have turned – every one – to his own way; and the Lord has laid on him the iniquity of us all". He continues, "It was the will of the Lord to crush him; he has put him to grief," and "by his knowledge shall the righteous one, my servant, make many to be accounted righteous, and he shall bear their iniquities" (Isaiah 53:5-6, 10-11). The blood of animals could not atone for sins, but the blood of the Son of God is mighty to save.

Jesus Christ was not just a carpenter from Nazareth. He was God made flesh. The very Living God took on humanity and lived among us. He taught us a better way, He showed us what love looked like, and He called us to repentance. Jesus did not relax the commandments of Moses. Rather, He intensified them! "You have heard that it was said to those of old 'You shall not murder; and whoever murders will be liable to judgment.' But I say to you that everyone who is angry with his brother will be liable to judgment; whoever insults his brother will be liable to the council; and whoever says, 'You fool!' will be liable to the hell of fire" (Matthew 5:21-22). Jesus said that! He reminded us that the standard was perfection, and therefore none of us could meet it. But He could, because He was no mere man. He was God made flesh.

His death was the cosmic sacrifice. The Lord taught us through centuries of Moses' Law that He would accept a perfect sacrifice in payment for sins. But until Jesus there was no acceptable sacrifice. The blood of Abel, the guilt of our sin, cried out for justice. It cried out for blood. And so God Himself decided to take the punishment. He, who owed nothing to the blood of Abel, freely gave His own life to die in our place, as a perfect sacrifice. And on Good Friday, the justice of God was satisfied and the cry of the blood of Abel was silenced. Now the blood of Jesus cries out a better word: Mercy! Mercy from the hand of God.

Now, you might ask how we know that this is true. How can we know that Jesus died as a sacrifice in our place? Well, in Matthew 27, it tells us that when Jesus hung from the cross there was darkness over all the land, and that when He died, crying out with a loud voice, there was an earthquake that split the rocks in two and the veil of the Temple was ripped from top to bottom. It was enough to convince the soldiers who had killed Him! "Truly," they said in Matthew 27:54, "this was the Son of God!"

But better than that, on Sunday morning, after Jesus had been buried and lain in the tomb, He rose from the dead. He came out of that tomb and appeared to His disciples, who went around the world, proclaiming the message of salvation down to this day. I declare that same message to you now.

In order to cover the sins of Israel, God made a Covenant with them. This was intended to teach them that no matter what standard they were held to, they would always fail, and that the blood of their failure required the shedding of more blood. All of this led to the coming of Jesus Christ, the Messiah, the Promised One. When He died on that cross, He fulfilled the promise of the Law and its sacrifices, and inaugurated a New Covenant between Man and God. He is the Mediator of that New Covenant. No longer are we tied to vain rituals. Instead, the Lord has offered us the atonement of sins freely, through the blood of His Son.

The Old Covenant was a temporary fix, but the New Covenant is a permanent solution. Whereas the Old Covenant required every sin to be paid for by the death of an animal, now there has been one sacrifice, once for all: the blood of Jesus that covers every sin. The Lord in His mercy offers you forgiveness of sins. Rather than writing on tablets of stone, God sends His Holy Spirit into our hearts to speak His Word. Rather than looking forward in desperation to a hope that may or may not come, we can look back with relief at Christ on the cross, and look forward to eternal life in Heaven.

What does it take to enjoy these blessings? Nothing but faith. It is the free gift of God, His grace given to you. God did everything that was necessary in order to bring you to Himself. Now all you need to do is come. Come and lay down your old self and let it die along with Jesus on the cross. Believe that what Christ did is enough to cover what you have done, and enter into the joy of knowing that you have been forgiven. And then you will receive the blessing of God's Holy Spirit, who will come into your heart to change not only the way you act, but the very thoughts and intentions of your soul. God wants to purge the heart of Cain from within you and lead you into a new, abundant life. It is an internal renewal, and it is available to you if you will come in humility.

CONCLUSION

Blood cried out for blood, so God offered His own. Justice has been satisfied. The blood of Abel lies at peace now, because the Son of God has paid the price. Now the blood of Jesus speaks a better word to us: Mercy! We are all in need of mercy. We all have sinned against God, and the motivation that causes us to sin still resides within our hearts. Tragically, that same sin will keep many people stubborn in their rebellion who refuse to receive the forgiveness of God. Hell awaits those who insist on paying their own penalty. But there is no need for that. "God so loved the world, that he gave his only Son, that whoever believes in him should not perish but have eternal life" (John 3:16).

God loves you. That's why He went to all this trouble in the first place. God would have been perfectly within His rights to end it all the minute Cain first slew his brother. But He didn't. Do you know why? Because He looked into eternity and saw you, and was filled with so much love for you that He determined to endure all the pain and shame of the cross so that He could save you from your own destruction. You fight and rage and shout to make yourself feel worthy. You may have even killed the Abel in your life, smashed the mirror that showed you who you really were. But God does not require that you be worthy, only that you let go of the sin that is holding you down like an anchor in the sea. His love is ready to save you – today.

Let me make one more interesting point. The very earth cried out to God because of the blood of Abel. We read of the earth groaning one other time. In Romans 8:19 it says, "The creation waits with eager longing for the revealing of the sons of God". The earth knows that until God's people are glorified, there is no hope. It waits for you. God Himself waits for you right now. Will you come and receive the gift that Jesus died to offer you?

6

The Liberty of Faith

The Resurrection

INTRODUCTION

On Friday, Jesus died on the cross. If it were anybody else, that would be the end of the story. But His life did not end with His death.

Jesus was crucified and buried on Friday, and lay in the tomb on Saturday, which was the Sabbath. But when the women came on Sunday to embalm His body, the Roman guard was gone, the stone was rolled away, and His body was missing. An angel appeared to them and said those immortal words, "He is not here, for he has risen" (Matthew 28:6)! That evening, the risen Lord appeared to His disciples for the first time. He would appear to them several times over forty days until His Ascension into Heaven.

Everything depends upon the Resurrection. As Paul explains in 1 Corinthians 15, "If Christ has not been raised, your faith is futile and you are still in your sins". Because Jesus has returned from the grave, we know that His sacrifice for our sins has been accepted, and He is able to deliver us from the grave as well. "If we have died with Christ, we believe that we will also live with him" (Romans 6:8). This is the source and assurance of all our joy as believers.

But one of the Lord's apostles did not believe at first. Poor Thomas, who has been forever stuck with the title of "Doubting Thomas". His story is sad, but it has a happy ending. Which is good news for us, because we are a lot like Thomas. We too have a hard time believing in that which we have not seen.

"Now Thomas, one of the twelve, called the Twin, was not with them when Jesus came. So the other disciples told him, 'We have seen the Lord.' But he said to them, 'Unless I see in his hands the mark of the nails, and place my finger into the mark of the nails, and place my hand into his side, I will never believe.' Eight days later, his disciples were inside again, and Thomas was with them. Although the doors were locked, Jesus came and stood among them and said, 'Peace be with you.' Then he said to Thomas, 'Put your finger here, and see my hands; and put out your hand, and place it in my side. Do not disbelieve, but believe.' Thomas answered him, 'My Lord and my God!' Jesus said to him, 'Have you believed because you have seen me? Blessed are those who have not seen and yet have believed.'" (John 20:24-29)

DOUBTING THOMAS

When Jesus first appeared to His disciples, Thomas was not with them. There could be any number of reasons why, the text does not explain. But it is clear that the Lord had a lesson that He still needed to teach Him. Thomas not only disbelieved the other apostles, he claimed that he would "never believe" unless he had absolute, indisputable proof.

Thomas had, as many of the other disciples did, a nickname. He was known as Didymus, which was Greek for "Twin". We only see him twice more in the Bible, both are in the book of John. The first case is when he "said to his fellow disciples, 'Let us also go, that we may die with him'" (John 11:16), when Jesus told them He was going to raise Lazarus from the dead. The other time is during the Last Supper, when Jesus told them He was going away. "Lord," said Thomas, "we do not know where you are going. How can we know the way?" (John 14:5). These stories are both expressions of skepticism. He doubted Jesus could survive a journey to Jerusalem, and he insisted on a clear statement of Jesus' destination. Unless he had the whole plan, he had a hard time believing.

We are in a similar position to Thomas the apostle. We have not seen the risen Jesus; all we have is the word of the apostles. For this reason, we see ourselves in Thomas. Like him, we are asked to take something wonderful on faith alone.

At this present time, doubt is considered to be a virtue. "Question everything!" scream the bumper stickers and YouTubers. The term "skeptic" has been elevated to mean "Intellectual" – or at least "smarty-pants". While I suppose there may be an appropriate place for such a sentiment, it is hardly a Christian one. Our religion is built upon faith. But there are even Christian writers and artists and pastors who have encouraged the Church in their doubts. There are church meetings that exist only to air the skeptical objections of the members, where no "answers" are allowed to be given. If that's not a scheme cooked up by the devil, I don't know what is!

Now, I would never be so insensitive as to deny the existence of doubts and questions. Questions about the existence of God, the Creation of the world, the inerrancy of Scripture, the Resurrection, and more – these are legitimate questions to ponder. But we have become just like the world if we act like Thomas and demand that each question be independently verified through the scientific method. Doubt is not a symbol of Christian maturity. We are to work through our doubts by the words of Scripture, the wisdom of other Christians and the inner quickening of God's Holy Spirit.

We are called to faith. And faith in what has already been proven is no faith at all. As we see in this story, choosing to hold on to your skepticism in the face of Christ is foolishness. Doubt leads only to misery, but simple faith brings liberty.

THE MISERY OF DOUBT

Imagine how deflated the other apostles must have been when Thomas did not believe. All their joy and exuberance would have turned into pity and frustration. For a while, anyway. I doubt they would have been able to hold in their excitement for long. So as the apostles spent a week praising God and wondering what was coming next, Thomas Didymus kept to himself and ignored them all. This is the misery of doubt.

Thomas today would be applauded as the only "rational" disciple, who refused to believe anything unless it had been sufficiently proven. But Thomas would have been the most miserable of this group of people. At any moment he could have changed his entire demeanor and entered into the same joy, but his doubts kept him out. The door was there before him, but the key to open it was belief, not evidence.

When Jesus had come to the disciples before, He said to them twice, "Peace be with you" (John 20:19, 21). Thomas had not yet received that peace, because he did not yet believe. In these verses, when Jesus arrives, He says again, "Peace be with you", but Thomas cannot receive it until he has cried out to Jesus in faith. Doubt leads to an inability to accept the peace of God.

Why is this so? There is no deficiency with God Himself. Jesus Christ is the Prince of Peace (Isaiah 9:6). Philippians 4:7 says that His peace "surpasses all understanding". The disconnect is with us. Isaiah 26:3 says, "You keep him in perfect peace whose mind is stayed on you, because he trusts in you". If we do not rest our minds on the truth of God and all that He has taught us, there is no peace for us, but turmoil. And this is not because your faith somehow "makes it real". God is real and Jesus has risen whether you believe it or not. But if you isolate yourself and begin making demands of God before you acknowledge His authority, your heart will have no access to the blessings that could be yours by faith.

Power in the spirit is based on faith. The miracles of Jesus were in proportion to the faith of the people. Salvation itself is received by faith. Faith in the truth. What is true about God is immensely powerful. The very idea of the Son of God crucified and risen from the dead speaks of incredible power. When we believe, we move out of the way and allow God to work. Faith lifts the sluice gate of the peace and power of God. Faith has no power on its own, but it is the valve that turns to release what's in the tank.

Therefore, the enemy, the devil, works to undermine faith in the truth. The opposite of the truth is a lie, and so lies are his primary weapon. Jesus called him "a liar and the father of lies" (John 8:44). If God's people believe a lie, they are powerless, because the effectual power of God is released through faith. And if Satan cannot get someone to believe an outright lie, instead he will introduce doubts in the truth. In the Garden of Eden, first he said, "Did God actually say, 'You shall not eat of any tree in the garden'?" (Genesis 3:1), and then he moved to the outright lie: "You will not surely die" (Genesis 3:4). These are his devices. Since there is power in belief, he works to undermine belief through doubts before introducing his lies.

You can see this in various stages throughout the world today. The existence of God, the inerrancy of Scripture, Creation, the Resurrection – all of them dead on the road that began with doubt. This is why we must deal with our doubts according to the Scripture, because doubts never hold their place. Faithlessness overflows the river of the mind and floods everything else. You cannot allow your doubts about the Resurrection or anything else to go unchallenged in your mind. It is not virtuous to have no answers to important questions

Doubts leave you miserable. You cannot fully enter into the joy of the Lord when your faith is weak. And if you let your doubts carry you away, you end up believing in nothing. All the wonderful truths of the Bible wash away, and you are left like Thomas: facing the misery of your life with nothing divine to hold on to.

I'll bet Thomas was growing bitter towards the fellow apostles. He resented them for believing when he did not, and he was probably jealous of their joy. But if he were to allow himself to envy them too much, then he would slip back down towards belief, and he could not accept that. So he hardened himself. Bitterness is a truly miserable place to be. Why do you think atheists and skeptics are the most vicious opponents of Christianity? What do they care if we believe in Jesus? If none of it's real, why bother mocking those who believe? Because they are left to view the world in all its horrors and uncertainties with none of the hope of the empty tomb. And so they hate us for daring to be so simple in our faith, and to guard themselves against the attraction of the Holy Spirit.

Doubt leads to misery. Look at the world around us. We have abandoned belief in God, and are we happier? Now that the Church has been driven out of public life and the academy, is there greater peace and harmony? No. We are killing ourselves in record numbers, and aimless young men open fire on young children in order to flout their despair and misery before the world. When doubt becomes not just a struggle, but a way of life, it undermines everything worth living for.

Until you can accept what Jesus has done by rising from the dead you will have no peace. It's easy to be a skeptic in a crowd, or online. But despite the mocking bravado of skeptics on the Internet, those same men wrestle with more depression springing from a lack of purpose than anyone else. It's more than memes – it's the misery of doubt.

THE INFERIORITY OF EVIDENCE

Now I have been speaking about doubts in a way that is sure to raise some eyebrows. To be clear: I do not believe that the claims of Christianity are groundless, and I do not believe that it is wrong to become mighty in the defense of the faith. However, in Matthew 12:39, when the Pharisees and scribes demanded a sign from Jesus to verify His claims, He said, "An evil and adulterous generation seeks for a sign". He condemned them for not believing the truth, regardless of whether they had sufficient evidence or not. The only sign He gave them was the Resurrection itself, and He shrouded that in symbolic language. It is not wrong to examine the evidence, but evidence is inferior to faith.

When the Lord finally appeared to Thomas, eight days later, He offered him the opportunity to verify the Resurrection personally. "Do not disbelieve," He said, "but believe". He offered him the exact kind of evidence that he had demanded. I find it remarkable that Thomas did not avail Himself of this opportunity but instead responded in faith. There's a lesson in that.

There are times when God will give us answers to our questions. Which reveals an important truth: there are answers to our questions! Thomas claimed he would only believe if he could touch the scars of Jesus. That was possible. Jesus could have arrived at any moment and allowed him to do just that. But if he had done so, it would have been a weaker step of faith for Thomas. Even now, we look at his faith as inferior – at least in that moment – to the other apostles.

There are answers to all those questions that we have. The Church has been pondering the big questions for centuries, and arriving at sufficient conclusions. Look at the Resurrection for example. We have eyewitness testimony recorded in a reliable contemporary manuscript. The history of the Church shows that they began preaching the

Resurrection at the very beginning; it did not come about gradually, as some have argued. How else do you explain the transformation of these timid souls, especially Thomas? A group hallucination? Hardly. Were they just liars? Not to the point of death they weren't!

Our culture has made a virtue of doubt. Americans and others in the West will not stand for insufficiently defended claims. And nowhere has this pressure been applied with greater force than to the Church. The assaults against God and His Bible are merciless. A higher standard of proof is demanded from Christians than from anyone else. And we have risen to the challenge, as I just explained. But somewhere along the line we have swallowed the world's starting premise: believing something on the basis of faith alone is unacceptable. This claim ought to set off alarm bells in your heart, because you are saved by faith alone (Ephesians 2:8). Not only do we disagree with this statement, we absolutely reject it.

God places a higher value on faith that does not see sufficient evidence of its object. In the Gospel of Luke, a Roman centurion asked for Jesus to heal his servant. Jesus offered to go to the man's house, but the old soldier said, in verse 7, "But say the word, and let my servant be healed". Jesus did not rebuke this man for being gullible, "He marveled at him, and turning to the crowd that followed him, said, 'I tell you, not even in Israel have I found such faith'" (Luke 7:9). Jesus commended faith that did not require proof – the exact opposite of what we have come to believe.

Why is this the case? Because what is true, is true! God will not relax His judgment on the final Day because someone was not exposed to the Ontological Argument before they died. He will judge with unwavering wrath because the wages of sin is death whether or not you agree. Smirking at the heavens and shouting, "Prove it!" at God does not make you wise, it makes you a fool. That is why Jesus sent us out not as skilled debaters of theology, but as proclaimers of the cross and the empty tomb.

Christian, if you can be argued into your faith, you can be argued out of it. One day, the proofs for the inerrancy of Scripture might seem overwhelming, but the next day all you can see are the holes. Fifty-one percent faith is not saving faith. And if you hang your hat on one single argument, say the latest archaeological discovery, you may find yourself one day without a leg to stand on. The more we rely on arguments and evidence instead of the supernatural power of God's living Word, the more we find ourselves tinkering with the Scriptures; re-evaluating doctrines not because of fresh light from the Holy Spirit, but because some heathen in a university said that we are not allowed to believe that anymore. Doubt always overflows its banks. Build your foundation on anything other than faith in God and His holy Word, and you build upon a foundation of sand.

I love apologetics. Paul said in 2 Corinthians 10:5, "We destroy arguments and every lofty opinion raised against the knowledge of God". Peter said in 1 Peter 3:15, "Always being prepared to make a defense to anyone who asks you for a reason for the hope that is in you". Throughout the centuries, the Church has fielded attacks from the outside; from the Romans, the Muslims and heretics of every stripe. But our foundation is not built upon these things. All these things can do is point back to what cannot be demonstrated in a laboratory – the saving work of Jesus Christ on the cross.

Jesus rebuked those who asked for signs. He preached in parables to obscure His message. Why? So that only those who sought God with a pure heart would be able to find Him. The salvation of the soul is a spiritual matter, not an intellectual one. God in His grace will provide evidence, and because His claims are true, the evidence will always be there. But as His disciples we believe in the inferiority of evidence when it comes to the matters of belief.

THE LIBERTY OF FAITH

The redemption of Thomas is a wonderful sight. He did not avail himself of the proofs when they were presented to

135

him, he only believed. And not only did he believe, but he went further than his brothers in making the great confession about Jesus: "My Lord and my God!" All of us have followed him in that example of faith since then. If Jesus Christ is risen, then Jesus Christ is Lord. He is God very God.

In that moment, it all came crashing over Thomas. All of his bitterness and doubt melted away. He saw that not even death could stop his Jesus. He knew that every word He ever said was true, every promise He ever made He would keep, and that this was a man – more than a man! – worthy of every breath and every ounce of strength he had left in his body. In John 20:28 he ceased to be doubting Thomas and became in truth the Apostle Thomas. One of the Twelve who led the Church in Jerusalem, missionary to the Indian peninsula, and faithful martyr for the name of His Lord and His God.

Do you see the freedom that came to his life when he was willing to let go and believe? This is the liberty of faith. Galatians 5:1 says, "For freedom Christ has set us free; stand firm therefore, and do not submit again to a yoke of slavery". When we stop treating the Bible as a term paper that needs to be graded; when we stop giving ourselves airs as some great intellectual; when we stop trying to impress people who hate God and His people; when we lift our eyes from the iPhone screen and look into the radiant face of the risen Christ – there! There is true freedom to be found. Try to prove your way into a man of faith, you will never do it. You will spend the rest of your life digging in the dirt to find one more scrap of evidence, hoping that some day you might be able believe. Don't do that! Just believe, and breathe in the first breath of real freedom outside the tomb of the skeptic.

I am firmly convinced that it is never the evidence that keeps people out of Heaven. And it is never the evidence that keeps people in the fold. Thomas did not really need to see the scars of Jesus to believe. That was just he had told himself in order to avoid facing the pain he had undergone when Jesus was killed. Thomas had slept while Jesus prayed in the Garden. He had fled when the soldiers came to arrest Him. If he saw the crucifixion at all, it was from a distance. Imagine the pain and the shame. He had barely been able to process it before he was faced with stories of His Resurrection. Could he risk opening up his heart to the possibility of more pain? Better to hide behind the mask of a skeptic in order to avoid facing the question. But when Jesus saw him face to face, and offered him His hands, Thomas would not dishonor his Lord and God with his own doubts. Knowing that Jesus was alive was enough to set him free.

That is what makes the difference. The issues that keep people out of the Kingdom are always deeply personal, not intellectual. Pain suffered perhaps at the hands of a Christian, or even a pastor. Fear of accepting the truth of Heaven and Hell, because that might mean a loved one has died without Christ. Pride and unwillingness to be seen as foolish before one's own peers or family. These are the things that make the difference.

That is why the job of apologetics is to move the conversation beyond the intellectual hurdles so that the evangelist can address the heart. Even if you were able to convince someone that abortion is wrong or that the New Testament is reliable, or even that Jesus rose again, what then? The New Testament might be reliable, but does that make it God's Word? Jesus may have risen from the dead, but why does that mean I ought to worship Him? Thomas could have claimed he was hallucinating or the other apostles had drugged him. The human mind, assisted by the schemes of the devil, is capable of moving the goalposts as far as is necessary.

Blaise Pascal said, "In faith there is enough light for those who want to believe and enough shadows to blind those who don't". We ought to answer serious objections, but aim straight for the heart. Open the conversation however you like, and then head for the cross. Proclaim the Word that never returns void (Isaiah 55:11), and then let the Holy Spirit do His work. Call people to faith, because that is where freedom is to be found.

Faith is an act of the will, choosing to believe what has been proclaimed. When you decide to believe in your heart and mind, you reach the end of the road to salvation. Some people may need to take a few detours to answer some questions, but the end is the same. There must be a decision to believe in what has been reported to you about God and the risen Jesus.

And it is only once you have done so that the proofs begin to click in your mind. The Scriptures come alive, the teaching of Jesus become sweet like honey in your mouth, and the Holy Spirit changes your very conscience within you. The whole Christian life is a testimony to the truth of the Resurrection, but it is something that only the Christian can experience. You have been in Church when the message speaks exactly to your situation; you have seen specific answers to prayer; you have had special experiences like dreams and miracles, haven't you? I have seen the Lord perform healings in answer to my prayers, and I tell you now that if I let my mind wander from that to the academic analysis of the Gospel, my step falters.

Your faith is not to be in a set of proven propositions, but in the living, risen Jesus Christ Himself. Simply choose to believe Him, and you will be rewarded with more experiential evidence than you could ever hope for.

The mire of endless arguments can be a swamp from which a Christian can never extract their rightful joy. Paul spoke of people who were, "always learning and never able to arrive at a knowledge of the truth" (2 Timothy 3:7). That ought not to be us. When will you finally have found enough evidence to consider yourself convinced? Some people wear themselves out watching videos and reading books and fighting online. It all looks to me like a profound lack of faith. It will weaken your own heart and ruin your evangelism. If you, as a Christian, cannot accept the simple truth of the Bible without buttressing it with ten thousand blogs and tidbits of information, what you need is not another seminar, but a good hour or three on your knees.

We must be able to consider interesting questions, even doubts, but then release them to enter into the joy of the Lord. When you come into the church building, there may be countless questions and even doubts running through your head. Ask the Lord to relieve the burden of your mind that you might worship Him. Put the words of faith in your mouth and declare what you believe to be true, regardless of the tempting questions of the adversary. Then what happens? Joy swells in your heart. You remember all that God has done for you, and the hope of eternity spent forever with Him. Now your doubts seem so small compared to His glory. You don't need to have every question answered perfectly, you know the most important thing: that Jesus is alive, and He's coming back for you someday!

The trick is to learn to do this all the time. This is why we need the discipline of daily devotions and prayer. Because you have a tempting serpent who whispers in your ear night and day. When you are in the Spirit, the world looks so small and unimpressive. So don't spend time outside of the Spirit. Walk in the Spirit and you will not fall prey to the fleshly arrogance of your mind.

Consider that first Easter Sunday. Just meditate on the glory of the Resurrection without entertaining the obnoxious complaints of unbelievers. Jesus Christ was the Son of God. He lived a sinless life and taught us how to live. He was betrayed by His own people and was nailed to a cross. He died and was buried in a borrowed tomb. Then on the third day, as dawn broke, the ground shook and the soldiers guarding it were knocked to the ground. An angel swooped down from Heaven in brilliant light with a celestial smile on his face. He rolled away that big old stone and out came Jesus Christ, scarred on His hands and feet, but alive – risen from the dead!

He died to pay the penalty for your sins, and He rose to give you new life. He ascended to Heaven at the right hand of the Father, where He intercedes and leads His Church until the Day when He will return in judgment to set all things right. And He will reign for 1,000 years upon the earth and destroy Satan at the final rebellion. Then the sky will be rolled up like a scroll and the earth shall flee away before the New Heaven and the New Earth, where we will live forever and ever and ever and ever and ever! That's the Gospel message that changed the world. That's the story that transformed my family and my life and gets me out of bed every single morning. "If you confess with your mouth that Jesus is Lord and believe in your heart that God raised him from the dead, you will be saved" (Romans 10:9). My sins have no hold over me anymore because Jesus has already paid the death penalty for them. I live not at the cross, but out of the empty tomb, in new abundant life by the Holy Spirit of God. That is the liberty of faith.

THE BLESSING OF BELIEF

Jesus said to Thomas as the end of our passage, "Blessed are those who have not seen and yet have believed". Peter spoke about this too in 1 Peter 1:8-9, "Though you have not seen him, you love him. Though you do not now see him, you believe in him and rejoice with joy that is inexpressible and filled with glory, obtaining the outcome of your faith, the salvation of your souls". We have not seen the risen Lord. All we have is the testimony of the apostles, just like Thomas had. And we are expected to believe based on that testimony. Each one of us has experienced God in various ways, and we are so super-educated that I am sure you have a working knowledge of most apologetics issues. But at the root of it, we must have faith, because we have not seen Him. And the Bible says there is a special blessing upon us for doing so.

We have become, in the Church, encultured to the world of the skeptic and the doubter. I am concerned that we have begun to believe the obvious lie that faith alone is insufficient for the thinking man. It has affected the way we speak, the way we sing, and the way that we preach. It has made us into Christians with thin souls.

People today are sick of cold skepticism. They are looking for something to believe in. They are not interested in proofs and arguments, especially in areas where science has no business sticking its nose anyway. Young people are rioting in the streets in a search for meaning and faith. The generations are shifting, and the throne of the scientist is being shaken from the bottom. We have the Gospel that can answer both the scientist and the social justice warrior, but if we tie ourselves too tightly to any one of these groups, we will be unable to reach the other. We cannot help anybody if we try to be just like them. We must reclaim the separation.

How do we do that? Brothers and sisters, can we not just be Christians? Can we not just believe the Bible because it is God's Word? Would it not be refreshing to speak of angels without cringing, or refer to Jesus as God without having to look over your shoulder? If we want to restore joy and vitality to our faith and to reach a desperate generation with the hope of the risen Jesus, then what we need is not a facelift or a re-interpretation. What we need is a little of that old-time religion.

If you are a Christian, you know that Christ is risen. You may not always be able to explain how you know, but you know it as sure as you know anything else. Embrace that mysterious certainty! it is the work of the Holy Spirit within you. It is not off-putting, as some would have you think – it is refreshing and appealing to those who are tired, "Prove it!"

As the old hymn says, "I need no other argument, I need no other plea. It is enough that Jesus died, and that He died for me."

CONCLUSION

And you know what's even better than that? Christ is risen! That is the greatest news I could ever give you. Because He is risen, He has opened up the door of salvation for all who believe. Thomas had a hard time believing at first, but when he finally did, it set his whole life at liberty. Don't be too clever and dilute your experience with God by dissecting it in a laboratory. Receive what He has done through faith, and live by that same faith every day. Get a little of that old-time religion in your life. Be content to be a Christian, and you will see the power of the risen Jesus fill your life with glorious liberty.

7

Fishers of Fishers of Men

The Great Commission

INTRODUCTION

"Now the eleven disciples went to Galilee, to the mountain to which Jesus had directed them. And when they saw him they worshiped him, but some doubted. And Jesus came and said to them, 'All authority in heaven and on earth has been given to me. Go therefore and make disciples of all nations, baptizing them in the name of the Father and of the Son and of the Holy Spirit, teaching them to observe all that I have commanded you. And behold, I am with you always, to the end of the age.'" (Matthew 28:16-20)

The final command of Jesus before His Ascension, as recorded in the Gospels is His commission to go into the world and make disciples. In essence, to go out by His unlimited authority and to start the Church. Everything that came after this, the coming of the Spirit at Pentecost, the early revival in Jerusalem, the persecutions, the missionary journeys, the cathedrals, the Reformation, even down to you and me today, was bound up in this Great Commission.

WHAT IS OUR MISSION?

It is very fortunate that Jesus, with "all authority", told us what we were to do after He was gone. Everyone has their own idea of what the Church ought to be. There are countless congregations around the world and throughout history that are living out some version of "church". And not all of them fall within what we would consider acceptable in the United States.

For example, when I was in Russia, I stepped into an Eastern Orthodox church during a service. The building was a hundred feet high, and inside there was no slide projector, no coffee stand and no one handing out bulletins. Instead, I was greeted with the smell of incense, a wall decorated with gilded paintings of the apostles, and a glass casket wherein I could see the bones of a dead saint. The ministers were not wearing suits or Hawaiian shirts, but black robes and turbans, with long grey beards. As strange as that sound to you and me, it is normal to millions of Christians around the world!

How are we to evaluate what is and is not acceptable in the Church? People have written books and dissertations on this subject. Every congregation has a mission statement, every seminary has a statement of faith, and everybody seems to feel free to weigh in! Even politicians, celebrities and the sages of social media have strong opinions on what the Church ought to be.

But I am only interested in what one Person has to say, and that is the risen Lord Jesus Christ. Paul wrote in Colossians 1:18, "He is the head of the body, the church". As He says in verse 18, "All authority in heaven and on earth has been given to me". This is His Church; we are His successors. I think it is only fair to let Him tell us what the Church is and what our mission ought to be.

There are four verbs, four action words in the Great Commission. Only one of these is an imperative, or a command. The three other verbs are participles, or verbal nouns. They describe how we are to go about obeying that one imperative. All three are important, but they are only to be done in service to the main command: to "make disciples".

For some people the mission of the Church is to "go"; a charitable mission. This is good, but insufficient.

For others the mission of the Church is "teaching"; a theological mission. This is better, but still insufficient.

For others the mission of the Church is "baptizing"; a social mission, and this is very, very close. But on its own it is insufficient.

The mission of the Church according to Jesus Christ, is to "make disciples". This is the commandment of the Great Commission, the goal that unites the others in true, biblical evangelism.

THE MISSION IS NOT CHARITY

The first verb of the Great Commission is, "Go". As I have just explained, this is a participle, grammatically subordinate to the main imperative. It might be translated "going", or "as you go". Our mission, true evangelism, is to involve a lot of "going".

In Acts 1:8, just before His Ascension, Jesus explained to the disciples, "You will receive power when the Holy Spirit has come upon you, and you will be my witnesses in Jerusalem and in all Judea and Samaria, and to the end of the earth". This is a rough outline for the whole book of Acts: the Church begins in Jerusalem, expands to Samaria by chapter 8, and ends with Paul in Rome on a mission to take the Gospel to the ends of the earth. Jesus mentioned here in verse 19 that we are to go to "all nations". We are here today in a nation farther away than any apostle even knew existed! The Church is to be a "going" Church.

There was a time when the Church did not think that it needed to be going anywhere. When William Carey, the famous British missionary to India, was seeking support for his journey, a wizened old man told him during the service, "Young man, sit down. If God sees fit to convert the heathen, He will do it without your help or mine". There are still those who want to gripe about Colonialism or Cultural Imperialism, but we're only interested in what Jesus had to say. And He said, "Go!"

When Jesus said to be going, it meant to take the life that He taught us to live and go live it somewhere else. In our culture the teachings of Jesus are respected and even imitated outside of the Church, but this is not the case everywhere. Jesus said, "Love your enemies, do good to those who hate you, bless those who curse you, pray for those who abuse you" (Luke 6:27-28). It is plain ignorance to believe this kind of love is valued in every culture. We've just gotten used to it. It is as radical to the Islamic, Hindu, Buddhist and secular nations now as it was to the Romans and Germanic tribes all those centuries ago.

This is why missions work, as it is called, has such an emphasis on charity and good works. Digging wells, providing medical care, distributing food and clothing to the needy – all of these things are essential. When Paul discussed his ministry with the apostles, they approved all his doctrine, "Only," Paul says in Galatians 2:10, "they asked us to remember the poor, the very thing I was eager to do". From its very beginning, the Church has gone around the world and lived out the love of God in Jesus' name. In every natural disaster it is Christian organizations that first spring into action to provide help and love in Jesus' name.

However, while charity is a good thing, and while we would be wrong to neglect it, charity is not the mission of the Church. Remember, "go" is one of the participles in this passage, it is subservient to the main mission. We should be creative and enthusiastic as we try to live out the life of Christ, but we must never let charity drive the bus.

A church that only "goes", that is – a church focused exclusively on charity – might do a lot of good, but it will not live up to the Great Commission. When Jesus fed the 5,000 by multiplying the loaves and fishes, they followed Him and said, "Sir, give us this bread always". But following that request in John 6, Jesus proceeded to give one of the most difficult teachings of His ministry, telling them that if they were hungry, they could eat His flesh and drink His blood. He refused to let good deeds become the focus of His ministry, the same reason why He would try to enter a

152

town quietly: if the requests for healings became overwhelming, He would have no chance to teach.

When the Church makes charity its primary mission, it begins to view other foundational principles as inconvenient. Christian charities, often of necessity, have broad doctrinal positions to attract as many helpers and donations as possible. But if the purpose is charity, why bother with doctrine at all? Why not let anyone help, even those from another religion? And if the purpose is charity – say, to end sex trafficking or dig wells – then why would the Church draw extra negative attention to itself by using the name of Jesus? It would be far easier to provide medical care in a Muslim country if you did not do so as a Christian. Better yet if you converted to Islam! Do you see the problem here? Ministries and churches that make charity the primary goal rather than a secondary goal have a tragic pattern of abandoning sound doctrine, minimizing the Gospel and even renouncing Jesus Christ.

Today there are so many groups that began as Christian ministries that have long since abandoned those roots. In many cases, unbelievers will volunteer because they see the Church as an effective vehicle for good deeds. And the Gospel becomes less and less of a priority. Consider the Red Cross, the YMCA or to a lesser extent the Salvation Army; groups that began as evangelistic outreaches but have long since made the transition to charitable programs. Any

153

church that does not build itself upon the death and resurrection of Jesus Christ for the forgiveness of sins is no true church. True evangelism requires more than that.

The wrong thing to do would be to forsake worldwide obedience and practical love in reaction to the errors of some. Charity is a good thing, it is part of the Great Commission, but on its own it is insufficient. Christ's Church is to be a "going" Church that takes the love of Christ around the world. But we must always remember that charity is not the mission, it is in service to the main mission.

THE MISSION IS NOT THEOLOGY

The third participle in the text, but the second we will consider is the word "teaching". As with the word "go" from the previous verse, this verb is a participle, subservient to the main verb of the Great Commission. The Church of Jesus Christ is to be a "teaching" Church.

It has become fashionable to say that the Bible is not all about having the right doctrine, but about loving people. This is wildly inaccurate, and ironically shows that there has not been enough teaching in that person's life. As Paul awaited his final execution, he wrote to his young protégé Timothy and charged him in 2 Timothy 4:2-4, "Preach the word; be ready in season and out of season; reprove, rebuke, and exhort, with complete patience and teaching. For the time is coming when people will not endure sound teaching, but having itching ears they will accumulate for themselves teachers to suit their own passions, and will turn away from listening to the truth and wander off into myths". The New Testament is full of passages like this, especially towards the end. Many of the epistles were written with the explicit purpose of correcting false doctrine or communicating sound doctrine.

1 Corinthians 4:1 calls us "stewards of the mysteries of God". We have the history of God's dealings with Israel, the prophecies and Psalms of the Old Testament, the Gospel of Jesus, and the instructive letters of the apostles. There is a lot to know as a Christian, and it is all important! Not only that, there is the grand tradition of godly men who have studied and interpreted and systematized the teaching of God's Word. Passing on this wealth of knowledge is profoundly important. That's why Paul required that every leader in every congregation must be "able to teach".

There is the teaching of sound doctrine. The pastors and teachers in the Church are to instruct the people about what they believe. Equally important is the correction of false doctrine. The devil is always at work to undermine the Church, and we must be on guard against that. Hopefully, by laying down a solid foundation of sound doctrine, the teacher can make his job of correction easier when trouble comes.

Jesus explains in verse 20 that we are to teach "all that [He has] commanded [us]". Paul said to the Ephesians in Acts 20:27, "I did not shrink from declaring to you the whole counsel of God". Nothing is to be left out when we teach. All sound doctrine comes from the Word. While there are great helps and resources available, I find myself plenty busy just teaching the Scriptures in our church! Nehemiah 8:8 is a model for how we teach: "They read from the book, from the Law of God, clearly, and they gave the sense, so that the people understood the reading". By teaching the whole Bible, the Church is not only inoculated against false teaching, but they are able to search the Word for themselves, and are not dependent upon any one teacher for their instruction.

However, the Church is not an academy. Teaching is not the sole purpose of Christ's Church. In this passage, "teaching" is a subsidiary aspect of the Great Commission, in service to the main mission. I love to teach and I love to study, but we must never make theology the drum marshal of the evangelism parade. A "teaching" Church is good – I would even say that it is better than an exclusively charitable Church, but Jesus did not send us out to be professors.

A Church that has made theology alone the purpose of its existence will not be an effective one. And there are churches like this. They invest all their time in doctrinal nuance and debate, with a high premium on reading and study. Maybe they're not academics, they're just hammering correct doctrine, week after week. But maybe they do have academic pretensions; they want to be known as intelligent and learned. "Knowledge puffs up," the Bible says, and that is exactly what happens to academy churches.

Two opposite things can happen. First, a church that has made theology the primary goal can become angry and feral. They turn the guns outward and they make the enemy anyone who disagrees with them. These churches are like YouTube comment sections when they come together. They are the First Church of the Right On, and everyone else must be cast down. Churches like this shrink into obscurity and yet become proud of their isolation.

The other extreme often happens in Bible colleges and seminaries. Christians who see theology as their sole mandate begin to worship theology as a god. They spend their lives studying and publishing the various aspects of Christian teaching. Then when they gain some attention, they start chasing that instead of the truth. They rub shoulders with other academics, and they start to see themselves as academics first instead of Christians. They become loose with their doctrinal standards because they

157

are so open-minded they cannot correct even themselves. Before long, somebody with wacky views and a strong personality causes the church or school to lurch away from the truth of the Word into speculation. They become the parrots of the world. This has been the story of almost every Christian college and university in the world, from Harvard and Princeton all the way down.

Jesus said to the people, "You search the Scriptures because you think that in them you have eternal life; and it is they that bear witness about me" (John 5:39). This tells us that it is possible to be very familiar with Christian teaching and yet be far away from Jesus Christ. By contrast, the blind man Jesus healed had only this to say: "Whether he is a sinner I do not know. One thing I do know, that though I was blind, now I see" (John 9:25). He knew nothing of the debates and academic literature of the time, but he knew Jesus! And that was enough. Theology is important, but it makes for an insufficient foundation.

Once again, the wrong thing to do would be abandon teaching altogether – and some have done exactly that. They have decided just to focus on contemporary issues or personal matters. Inevitably, though, they drive off a cliff because they have no compass. We've got to teach all the way through the Bible, and then teach through it again. We need to address dangerous errors and thoughtfully consider the words of godly men.

Because theology and teaching is such a good thing, it is a real temptation to put it on the throne. But our mission is not theology and teaching; it is only to be in service to the main mission of evangelism.

THE MISSION IS NOT COMMUNITY

The third participle in these verses is "baptizing". The Church is to be a "baptizing" Church; we are to be making converts. As you have probably guessed by now, this is also subservient to the main imperative. Of the three, this is the one that is closest to the real mission, and at times can even be mistaken for real evangelism. But as we will see, it too is to be in service to our actual goal.

Acts 2:47 says, "And the Lord added to their number day by day those who were being saved". Baptism is the Christian rite of initiation. Making converts, adding people to the church is a worthy endeavor, and one that we should be pursuing at all times. I laugh at those who rail against large churches, because the early Church began on its first day with more than 3,000 people! And not long after they added thousands more. Jesus Himself attracted large crowds of people, and the disciples baptized them (John 4:1). If we are doing the work well, we should expect that souls will be added to the Church.

See how Jesus tells us to baptize them in the name of the Father, the Son and the Holy Spirit. We are bringing these people into fellowship with God, and therefore into fellowship with us. The Church is one big family. Even the world can see the value in the community of Church. A big group of people aiming towards the same goal can be a great motivator. Growing churches can transform neighborhoods, cities and nations.

But! As was true with charity and theology, the goal of the Church is not community. Our purpose is not to build a community. Not even a wholesome, family-friendly one. This is very close to the main goal, but it is not. Even making converts and growing the church is not the ultimate mission of Christ's Church. This may seem like splitting hairs, but Jesus said it this way for a reason.

When the crowds were massing around Jesus, being baptized by His disciples and swearing to follow Him wherever He went, the disciples were ecstatic. But Jesus, it says in John 2:24, had a different attitude. "Jesus on his part did not entrust himself to them, because he knew all people." How many times did Jesus teach us that not everyone who says, "Lord, Lord!" will enter the Kingdom of Heaven (Matthew 7:21)? Think of the parable of the sower and the rocky and thorny soil. Think of the wheat and the tares. He prophesied that the Church would grow alright; many, many people would be baptized and initiated. But He knew that there would be bad fish among the good, and wolves among the sheep. That is why our ultimate goal cannot merely be to add to our numbers. The Church is not just a society or a community.

A church that is only focused on building a large community will do many things right. These are hardworking churches. They strategize and plan and test ideas. They involve as many people in the church as possible to help. They have beautiful buildings and dynamic worship music, and their websites are the envy of just about everybody. None of that is wrong! The Lord is worthy of all those things. The problem is that they are often done at the expense of depth and vitality.

A community church will focus everything on building up the organization, especially on the front end. Much of the funding and energy goes into the experience of the visitor and streamlining the process of getting them committed. But because of this, the preaching is aimed at a lower level and the people do not grow. Little attention is given to doctrinal instruction or personal accountability, and many troublemakers and hurting people hide in the ranks. Everything becomes based on market research and technique rather than the Gospel and the Bible, and leaders are allowed to take prominent places because of business acumen rather than their spiritual maturity.

Now, all of these things can be overcome! We should not throw out all the great things we can learn from rapidly growing churches, but we must never let the goal of a great community drive the bus. We want to be "baptizing", making converts and growing the church. But that is not the most important thing. It is only partial evangelism. The mission of the Church is not to baptize as many people into the community as possible. The American Church in particular is held under the sway of this insufficient emphasis; it affects all of us. May the Lord deliver us from lesser things!

THE MISSION IS EVANGELISM

So then, the mission of the Church is not charity – we are not only to "go" and do good works; it is not theology – we are not only to be "teaching"; and it is not even to build a great community – we ought to be "baptizing", but there is more. All of these things are good; we should do all of them. But in these verses, they are participles attendant to the main verb. There are four verbs in this passage, and only one of them is an imperative, a command. Everything else is to be in service of this goal. And that goal is to "make disciples". We have been sent out by Jesus to make disciples. That is true evangelism, the fulfillment of the Great Commission.

We use that word "evangelism", and we tend to associate it with making converts, as we just discussed, but that is only the first step in making a disciple. The word "evangelize" in Greek comes from the prefix *eu*, which means "good", the word *angelion*, which means "message", and the ending *izo*, which we transliterate to "ize". Put way too literally, evangelize means "good-news-ize". It is not just the proclamation of the message, but the transformation of an entire life in response to the Good News about Jesus. We are to go out and Gospel-ize people, cities, and the whole world.

And the way we do that is to make disciples. To make a disciple goes beyond initiation. It means to take responsibility for bringing somebody into Christian maturity. A disciple is someone who "disciplines" themselves to follow a certain person or way of life. It is a lifelong process to become a disciple, and our job as Christians is to cultivate that process in other people. Paul said in Ephesians 4:13 that the leaders of the Church should be training and teaching the congregation, "until we all attain to the unity of the faith and of the knowledge of the Son of God, to mature manhood, to the measure of the stature of the fullness of Christ". This cannot be done in an afternoon or over a few weeks, it is like taking on an exchange student or adopting a child. The goal is to produce a mature, self-sustaining disciple.

Jesus gave us the example through the way He made His Twelve disciples. Mark 3:14-15 says, "And he appointed twelve (whom he also named apostles) so that they might be with him and he might send them out to preach and have authority to cast out demons". There are a few things here. He called them to be "with him". They were to be around Him all the time so that they could learn by watching Him and interacting with Him. This is why we come together as a congregation and ought to spend time with one another often. It is great to be taught the principles, but we need to see it done. We need someone who can tell us simply, "Do it this way". And Jesus also chose them that He might "send them" out. This was the training part; there was always a goal. He did not want them to remain in their infancy, but to go out and do as He did. We do not gather disciples around us like trophies, but we release them to do the work. This means giving them real chances both to fail and to succeed, so that we can help them do better next time.

Paul made disciples all over the Mediterranean Sea. Reading through Acts, we get the impression that Paul moved around a lot. This is true, but the condensed narrative makes it seem faster than it was. Paul stayed for a year and a half in Corinth, and three years in Ephesus. He wrote them letters and would return to check on their progress. He was willing to stay as long as it took for each church to stand on their own two feet. When he was chased out of Thessalonica after only a short time, he sent Timothy back to check on them with a letter saying, "We pray most earnestly night and day that we may see you face to face and supply what is lacking in your faith" (1 Thessalonians 3:10). He also set an example by the way he trained up men who could do what he did: Timothy, Silas, Titus, Aristarchus, Epaphroditus, and Luke. They traveled with him, learned from him, served alongside him, and eventually he sent them out to do it on their own. He taught them to know God, not to rely on his instructions. Paul was not just making converts, he was making disciples.

Jesus was able to send out the Twelve, Paul was able to send out Timothy to Ephesus and Titus to Crete and all the others. They did not do everything themselves, they focused on building up good people who could work alongside them. Our attitude is to be like that of Jesus in John 14:12, "Whoever believes in me will also do the works that I do; and greater works than these will he do". The goal of making a disciple is to train up somebody who is as mature and capable as you are – or more! It is the Gospelization of a person's life. We are to oversee the permeation of the Christ-life into every aspect of a person.

This is not just for pastors and apostles, this is the Great Commission. It applies to everyone. I have learned in ministry that it is far better to focus on the few who are absolutely committed than to try and drag forward the reluctant. No matter how capable a person is or what their background might be, if they are willing to leave all to serve Christ, God can make a disciple out of them. Paul said in 2 Timothy 2:2, "What you have heard from me in the presence of many witnesses entrust to faithful men who will be able to teach others also". When I have trained up two or three or twelve solid disciples, I have just multiplied myself. Now I can move on to make other disciples, and they can do the same thing. This is the only biblical way to build up a church, not just through adding more people to fill the seats, but by multiplying disciples who multiply disciples.

This is the imperative of the Great Commission. To "make disciples". To invest in the lives of those who have been born again in order to raise them up to maturity in Christ. This is harder, it takes longer and it does not make for flashy results. But it is what Jesus did. It is what the Twelve did. It is what Paul did. It is what John Wesley and D.L. Moody, and Chuck Smith did. And it is what our Bibles tell us we are to do as well. The mission of the Church is evangelism – real, disciple-making Gospel-ization of one life after another.

BRINGING IT ALL TOGETHER

Now that we know the goal, we can put the other elements in their proper place. If we know that the goal of real evangelism is to make disciples who will make disciples, then these other things come alive. We never let them take over, but we do them in service to the main goal. When we put it all together, that's the Great Commission.

As we seek to make disciples, we are to be "going". We are to spread out throughout the whole world and live out the love of Jesus. Now we know what all that charity is for! We don't just dig wells or provide vaccines because it's nice to do, we do it as part of the evangelistic mission. Our good works are like Jesus' miracles. They are a demonstration of sincere love and a desire to help. They adorn the message so that people will listen. And they show the new disciples what it really looks like to love people. Done this way, good works have their proper place, and we are no longer in danger of becoming just another humanitarian agency.

As we seek to make disciples, we are to be "teaching". There is a worldwide drought of the knowledge of God, and we have the solution right here in our hands. But teaching is not a goal unto itself. We teach in order to make disciples. We never hoard knowledge for ourselves, we teach the whole counsel of God to every Christian. And we never patronize those we think are somehow beneath us; we give them everything, from the famous stories to the Hypostatic Union. It is all important. We are trying to make self-sustaining disciples. So we do not hitch them to our wagon,

167

we seek only to attach them to the Word of God. That way they will stay faithful long after we are gone.

And as we seek to make disciples, we are to be "baptizing". Like the great examples in the book of Acts, we make an appeal to the souls of all men. We are not just focused inward, we are focused outward, proclaiming the message and seeking to add to our numbers in the best possible sense. We are not looking for a higher number on the attendance chart, but we know that each new visitor is a potential new disciple who can make more disciples. This also affects the methods we use to try to "bring them in", because we are not looking for a quick hand in the air, but a lifelong commitment. The ministry of evangelists like Billy Graham is to go around the world scattering seeds, but our job is to take the new little saplings and cultivate them in the Church to become mighty oaks with seeds of their own.

Do you see how making disciples redeems all these other things? They have purpose and life now. If we let the Church get out of balance, we are settling for something less than the Great Commission of Jesus Christ. He knew what would be effective and what would bear lasting fruit. Jesus helped a lot of people, but where were they in the Upper Room on Pentecost? He taught a lot of people, He even baptized a lot of people (or His disciples did). But when the Spirit came, there were only 120 out of the thousands who had shouted "Hosanna!" on Palm Sunday. His disciples endured to make more disciples, who made more disciples until here we are today – making disciples!

This is real evangelism, real Gospel-ization. This is how you take back what the devil has stolen. When you make a disciple, you are not just getting a person to switch religions, you are helping them reclaim their passions, their relationships and their priorities for the Kingdom of Christ. You are helping them to know God. Jesus said to Peter in Matthew 16:18, "I will build my church, and the gates of hell shall not prevail against it". Gates are defensive. In this metaphor, the Church is on offense. I had a professor who used to say, "Kick some gate!". Making disciples is how we slowly but surely secure each new beachhead as we storm the gates of Hell.

CONCLUSION

During the recent War on Terror, the Department of Defense, impressed with the effectiveness of the Special Forces, ordered more. They demanded that more candidates be approved, and the requirements were lowered in order to produce more Rangers and elite Recon units. Only the Navy SEALs refused to lower their standards. They knew that to reduce the requirements might result in more SEALs, but the quality of each man, and therefore of each team, would suffer, jeopardizing the effectiveness of the whole operation.

In the same way, real evangelism does not stop when a person bows their head, closes their eyes and comes down the aisle. That is only the first step. Evangelism is the act of making disciples, training new elite soldiers to fight in the battle for the Lord's army. We cannot do this quickly, it is a lifelong process in which we all must participate.

We are fishermen who teach the fish to fish for other fish!

You are not just spectator or a client of the Church. You are a disciple of Jesus! You have committed your life to learn what He taught and to live how He lived. You have a relationship with Him in a personal way. Is there anything more important than that? You should always have someone more mature in the faith than who can instruct you. Going it alone is a terrible idea. Don't "make it your own", find someone who can show you what to do. And then find someone who is less mature in their faith than you, and make a disciple out of them. You may feel unqualified, but we learn by doing. You may only know ten things about the Gospel – Well, find someone who only knows nine, and then teach them number ten! This is how the Church grows. Our roots grow deeper and deeper until the branches are strong and heavy with fruit, able to withstand any onslaught in the power of God's Holy Spirit.

Everything else is inferior to this. We are to be "going" and showing the love of Jesus in practical ways, but always with the goal of making disciples. We are to be "teaching", instructing people in the truth of God and His Word, but always with the goal of making disciples. And we are to be "baptizing" new converts and adding to the Church, but always with the goal of making disciples. These other things can be dangerous if they are allowed to take first place. But properly situated in their supporting role, they become invaluable.

Jesus ends His Great Commission by saying, "Behold, I am with you always, to the end of the age". If we will go about the business of the Church His way, Jesus will be with us. How foolish of us would it be to ditch the mission He gave us and then holler at Him to keep up and bless us? No, let us do it His way. We are to be evangelists, on a mission to make disciples, going, teaching and baptizing. With all authority in Heaven and on earth, this is what Jesus told us to do. So let's be about the work of making disciples who will make disciples, because if we do, then Jesus will be with us, even "to the end of the age".

171

8

His Work Continues

The Ascension

INTRODUCTION

When we think of the Gospel, we usually think of the death and resurrection of Jesus. And that is a good thing! We look back to the story of what He has done, and we look forward to what He will do when He returns. But what about today? What is Jesus doing right now? We know He is going to return, so that implies that He went somewhere, right? We cannot end a study of the final days of Jesus without looking at the bridge between the cross and the

Church.

Mark tells us the story: "So then the Lord Jesus, after he had spoken to them, was taken up into heaven and sat down at the right hand of God" (Mark 16:19).

This event, the Ascension of Jesus, is as significant for us as Christmas, Good Friday and Easter. All the claims of the Christian faith, from forgiveness to comfort to power for holy living, are possible only because Jesus ascended to Heaven.

In 1 Timothy 3:16, Paul gives a quick creed, a rapid-fire Gospel that culminates in the Ascension: "God was manifested in the flesh, justified in the Spirit, seen by angels, preached among the Gentiles, believed on in the world, received up in glory." For Paul, the Ascension of Jesus was the crowning moment of the story of salvation. The New Testament makes much of the exaltation of Jesus Christ, and so should we.

There is a rich vein of spiritual gold to be dug out of this doctrine. To study the Ascension is to gaze upon the incredible possibilities that have been opened up to us as Christians. I hope that our faith will be built up to seek the Lord, that we might realize these promises in our everyday lives.

ANTICIPATION OF THE ASCENSION

There are many doctrines that hinge on an exalted Christ, but let's start with something much simpler: God promised that Christ would ascend. He said it before, during and after His ministry. Unless God is a liar (He's not – Titus 1:2), we are compelled to believe that Jesus' destiny was always to return to the right hand of the Father.

The Ascension was prophesied in the Old Testament. It anticipates the Ascension as the culmination of the Messiah's mission. Psalm 110 says in verse 1, "The Lord said to my Lord, 'Sit at My right hand, till I make Your enemies Your footstool.'" And then in verse 4, "The Lord has sworn and will not relent, 'You are a priest forever according to the order of Melchizedek.'" This psalm was a favorite of the early Church. It's quoted in the book of Acts, Paul's epistles, Peter's epistles, and especially in Hebrews. Written a thousand years before the birth of Jesus, this psalm describes the Messiah sitting down at the Lord's right hand. Obviously, this could not refer to David, since David did not ascend to the heavens, and he certainly never became a priest. But it foretold that the Son of David would one day sit at the right hand of God. That He would receive authority there to rule the world and to intercede as a high priest on behalf of His people.

So, as good students of the Bible, we should expect that

the Christ would not only die and rise again, but would ascend to Heaven in great glory. Of course, Jesus claimed to be the Christ. If that is true, then we should expect this exaltation to be part of His story. Sure enough, His return to Heaven was something Jesus discussed frequently.

"Let not your heart be troubled," He said, "You believe in God, believe also in me. In My Father's house are many mansions; if it were not so, I would have told you. I go to prepare a place for you. And if I go and prepare a place for you, I will come again and receive you to Myself; that where I am, there you may be also. And where I go you know, and the way you know" (John 14:1-4)

Here, at the Last Supper, Jesus is comforting His disciples. He had told them He was going away, but He promises to return for them. Thomas asks the question on all our minds: "Lord, we do not know where You are going, and how can we know the way?" (John 14:5). Where was Jesus going? "Jesus said to him, 'I am the way, the truth, and the life. No one comes to the Father except through Me" (John 14:6). Jesus was going back "to the Father".

The Scriptures prophesied the Messiah's Ascension, and Jesus claimed that He would ascend to the Father too. He even promised to take others with Him. This appears more and more important, doesn't it?

After Jesus rose from the dead, He appeared to Mary Magdalene outside of the empty tomb, the first person to see Him after He rose. He said, "Do not cling to Me, for I have not yet ascended to My Father; but go to my brethren and say to them, 'I am ascending to My Father and your Father, and to My God and your God'" (John 20:17). The first thing Jesus said to anybody after His Resurrection was about the impending Ascension! He spent 40 days appearing to many witnesses, and this was one of the primary things He wanted to talk about. His work on earth was coming to a wondrous conclusion, and He wanted the disciples to know what was coming next.

So the Old Testament prophesied it, Jesus spoke of it before His death, and after His Resurrection, He made it a priority. That's what all of this amounts to: the Ascension is a biblical priority. This was why Jesus came to earth in the first place – that He might return to God's right hand with Man's salvation secured.

Here's another New Testament creed that emphasizes the Ascension: "He is the radiance of the glory of God and the exact imprint of his nature, and he upholds the universe by the word of his power. After making purification for sins, he sat down at the right hand of the Majesty on high, having become as much superior to the angels as the name he has inherited is more excellent than theirs" (Hebrews 1:3-4). Actually, if we want to be pedantic, these verses celebrate the Session of Christ, that He "sat down at the right hand of the Majesty on high". Ascension is the going up, Session is the sitting down. Usually we discuss these things as one event.

Put very plainly, the Gospel is incomplete without the Ascension. We know this because the Bible insists upon it before, during, and after the life of Jesus. And Scripture's priorities should be our priorities.

WHAT HAPPENED?

Let's discuss the mechanics, so to speak, of the Ascension. What actually took place on that day? Mark 16:19 gave us the short version, but the book of Acts gives us a few more details.

"Now when He had spoken these things, while they watched, He was taken up, and a cloud received Him out of their sight. And while they looked steadfastly toward heaven as He went up, behold, two men stood by them in white apparel, who also said, 'Men of Galilee, why do you stand gazing up into heaven? This same Jesus, who was taken up from you into heaven, will so come in like manner as you saw Him go into heaven.'" (Acts 1:9-11)

We can begin from a physical standpoint. Jesus ascended from a place to a place. He started on the Mount of Olives, then He went up to Heaven. We know by this that Heaven is a physical place. Otherwise, Jesus could not have ascended in His body. This is not to say that we could fly to

Heaven if we had the coordinates! But as Paul says in 1 Corinthians 15, those in Heaven have "heavenly bodies" or "spiritual bodies". Jesus ascended to Heaven bodily; He is no mere spirit.

This brings us to a very important point concerning the nature of Christ: the Hypostatic Union is eternal. That may sound strange to you, but that little sentence conceals a depth of glory. Let's let Paul explain it, and then we'll come back and define some terms.

"Christ Jesus...though he was in the form of God, did not count equality with God a thing to be grasped, but emptied himself, by taking the form of a servant, being born in the likeness of men. And being found in human form, he humbled himself by becoming obedient to the point of death, even death on a cross. Therefore God has highly exalted him and bestowed on him the name that is above every name, so that at the name of Jesus every knee should bow, in heaven and on earth and under the earth, and every tongue confess that Jesus Christ is Lord, to the glory of God the Father." (Philippians 2:5-11)

In eternity past, the Son was the divine second person of the Trinity. "The Word was with God and the Word was God," John said (John 1:1). But when the Son became a man named Jesus, He "emptied Himself". We call this the Kenosis, the "emptying" of the Son – not of His divinity, that would be impossible. He emptied Himself of His glory

179

and His divine privileges. The Son of God took upon Himself the body and nature of a man. That's not just poetry, He literally became a man. We call this the Incarnation, the "in-body-ment" of Jesus.

When we say, "Hypostatic Union", that's what we're talking about. The old word *hypostasis* means "substance" or "essence", the absolute nature of something. Jesus was, and remains, 100% God and 100% Man. He was in the "form" (*morphe*) of God but took the "form" (*morphe*) of a servant. Whatever He has as God, He now also has as Man. That is how He could accomplish what He did at the cross. Because He was a man He could die, and because He was God He could die for everyone.

During His time on earth, Jesus lived as a man. He never used His power to serve Himself (Matthew 4:3-4). But when Jesus returned to Heaven, did He shed His humanity and step back into divinity alone? No! The Son continues forever in solidarity with Man. He did not jettison His humanity at His Ascension. Long after, Paul would still refer to him as "the man Christ Jesus", the only possible mediator between God and men (1 Timothy 2:5). He remains fully human, and therefore is able to continue His redemptive work.

But now that He is glorified, He makes full use of His divine privileges again. He took up again the glory He had shared with His Father from before the foundations of the world (John 17:5). And that glory is now supplemented by

His rights as the God-Man. Which means that at this very moment there is a Man seated at the right hand of God with all power and authority. Let that sink in for a while! The second person of the Triune Godhead is, by His own sovereign will, eternally bound to humanity.

He existed in eternity past as God very God. Then out of love He emptied Himself (Kenosis) and became a Man (Incarnation). When this God-Man had accomplished His work of redemption He returned to Heaven (Ascension) and sat down at the right hand of God (Session). That's what happened that day – the Son returned to the Father, bearing humanity with Him into the heavenly places.

But what exactly is He doing up there? Jesus Christ is not idle in Heaven. In fact, His ministry has expanded beyond our wildest expectations. I'd like now to look at the work that Jesus does now that He has ascended. Every one of these things is crucial for the Christian life, and not one of them would be possible apart from the Ascension.

MEDIATING SALVATION

We read earlier from Psalm 110:4, where it prophesied that the Messiah would be "a priest forever according to the order of Melchizedek". This first work of Jesus is the most important: He is mediating salvation as our heavenly High Priest. While everything necessary for salvation was completed on the earth, at God's right hand Christ executes the completed work of the cross.

A priest is a go-between for God and men. The priest has a foot in both worlds, the secular and the sacred. He represents God to the people, and he represents the people to God. The Law is full of detailed descriptions of the work of the priests.

Jesus fulfills that role for us now. He is our go-between. Like a priest, He has a foot in both worlds, although to a far greater degree. He represents God to us, as the one worthy of all praise and worship. And He represents us to God. He is the only mediator, Paul said. A high priest's job is to provide covering for sin, and that's what Jesus does as our High Priest. Not a son of Aaron, qualified according to the flesh, but of the order of Melchizedek – qualified by the power of an "indestructible life" (Hebrews 7:16)

Jesus ascended to Heaven to mediate salvation. How would the priests mediate atonement for sins under the Law? By offering sacrifices. And Jesus has offered the greatest sacrifice of all, His very own body. His blood, not the powerless blood of bulls and goats, was shed at the cross. As the old song says, "There's power in the blood!" His willing sacrifice satisfied the wrath of God for you and for me. We couldn't do that ourselves. Psalm 49:7-8 says, "Truly no man can ransom another, or give to God the price of his life, for the ransom of their life is costly and can never suffice." Only the perfect, divine-yet-human, blood of Jesus could serve as an acceptable covering for sin.

Under the Old Covenant, a sacrifice had to be made for every sin. But Jesus offered Himself once for all. And when a man or woman comes to Him in repentance and faith, He applies that sacrifice to them. He mediates between them and God, verifying that their sins have indeed been paid for by the sacrifice He made. It is not a repeated sacrifice, but a renewable blessing that never runs dry!

So what does Jesus do all day? He washes souls in His blood! He writes their name in His Book of Life, which He will present to the Father at the final Judgment (Revelation 20:12). What joy must fill the Lord's heart as He stands before His Father on our behalf! Every day, more and more people receive the benefits of His blood, His death counting for their own. And He is the only one qualified to execute this office.

"Seeing then that we have a great High Priest who has passed through the heavens, Jesus the Son of God, let us hold fast our confession. For we do not have a High Priest who cannot sympathize with our weaknesses, but was in all points tempted as we are, yet without sin. Let us therefore come boldly to the throne of grace, that we may obtain mercy and find grace to help in time of need." (Hebrews 4:14-16)

If you have put your faith in Christ Jesus, then He is

your High Priest and mediator before God the Father. His blood has covered every sin, there is no more wrath awaiting you in God's presence. We need not hide from the face of God, there is no more condemnation awaiting us there (Romans 8:1). When Jesus died on the cross, the veil of the Temple was rent in two, because the way to God had been opened.

The grace of God does so much more than just forgive your sins. You are now granted access to the Lord to find "help in time of need". You remember the story of Esther? She could not simply approach the king, but had to wait for his summons and for him to extend his royal scepter (Esther 4:11). The same is true for you and me. We could not come to God because of our sin. Yet Christ has ascended to Heaven with everything necessary to open the doors. You have all the rights of a son or daughter to approach the throne of Heaven because of Christ's ongoing, mediating work as our great High Priest.

INTERCEDING ON OUR BEHALF

Closely tied to that first work is the second. Not only does Jesus perform a single act of mediation, He continuously intercedes on our behalf. The writer to the Hebrews said, "He always lives to make intercession" (Hebrews 7:25).

What is intercession? It means to intervene on behalf of somebody else. Your initial justification was a work of intercession. But Hebrews 7:25 reminds us that this is something that continues. Every day, Jesus Christ stands before God to advocate for you. Quite literally, Jesus is praying for you all the time! Within the mystery of the Trinity, it has always been the role of the Son to ask and receive from the Father (John 11:42). And with all the heavenly rights and privileges of the Son of God, He sticks up for you day by day.

This is important for us, because we also have an accuser in Heaven. The name, Satan, is a Hebrew name that means "adversary", as in a court of justice. We would call such a person a prosecutor today. We see this in the early chapters of the book of Job, where Satan appears before God and insists that Job's faithfulness was only because of his blessings.

Satan has no power over your soul; he cannot drag you to Hell. His strategy is to come into the courtroom of Heaven and accuses you to God and demands that God execute His justice. This is a terrifying thought, because we know that we are guilty! There is no hope of getting off on a technicality or asking for clemency. "As it is written, 'None is righteous, no, not one'" (Romans 3:10).

But now Jesus has returned to Heaven, where He performs His priestly duties. And now that our sins have been covered by His blood, the justice of God has been satisfied. So when Satan comes in to accuse you, you do not stand alone. You have a divine Defense Attorney! John said in that famous verse, "If anyone sins, we have an Advocate with the Father, Jesus Christ the righteous" (1 John 2:1).

We see a very clear picture of this in Zechariah 3:1-5. The prophet has a vision of Joshua the high priest, representative of the returned exiles. He stands before God in filthy rags, and Satan is there accusing him. You can imagine the Devil calling out Israel's idolatry and bitterness and hypocrisy. But then the Lord Himself rebukes Satan, saying, "Is this not a brand plucked from the fire?" Point being – I have chosen to save this man and the people he represents, so your accusation has no place here! And Zechariah watches as Joshua is clothed with "rich robes" and the Lord says to him, "See, I have removed your iniquity from you".

That is what happens every day in Heaven. Satan comes to accuse you before God. He holds up your rap sheet with all your lies and lusts and laziness on it and demands that the Father send you to everlasting fire. But Jesus steps in and says, "Father, we've already handled this case! My blood covers him, so the penalty has been paid." Imagine the impotent rage on Satan's face as the case is dismissed yet again. Someday the accuser will be thrown down for good (Revelation 12:10), but in the meantime, the ascended

Christ is there to stand in the gap for you.

And this expands beyond matters of Heaven and Hell. Romans 8:34 says that Christ Jesus "is at the right hand of God, who indeed is interceding for us". This is an ongoing ministry. By the way, Romans 8:26-27 says that the Holy Spirit prays for you, too!

How might Jesus intercede for you? Consider your life. You don't know what you need, but Jesus does. You don't know which job or relationship would be best, but Jesus does. When trials and tribulations come, sometimes you feel too weak to pray, but Jesus never is. And while you sometimes lose sight of your sanctification, Jesus is always focused on what is best. How effective is prayer when the very one in whose name you pray is saying "Amen" right along with you?

At the Last Supper, Jesus told Simon Peter, "Simon, Simon, behold, Satan demanded to have you, that he might sift you like wheat, but I have prayed for you that your faith may not fail. And when you have turned again, strengthen your brothers" (Luke 22:31-32). That's what goes on in the invisible. Satan comes in to accuse you, to demand the right to test you. And Jesus is there, praying you through those situations.

Like Jesus said to the woman caught in adultery, "Where are your accusers?" (John 8:10). When you feel like God is angry with you, and every thought is an internal accusation

– that does not come from Jesus, He is our Advocate. Satan is the accuser. Don't listen to his lies, instead demand to know how he dares to bring a reviling accusation against the one God has chosen to save! Every accusation falls flat before the intercession of our great Advocate.

SENDING HIS HOLY SPIRIT

I mentioned the Holy Spirit a moment ago, so that's where we'll direct our attention next. One of the main reasons Christ ascended was so that He could send His Holy Spirit.

Maybe you're wondering why Jesus ascended in the first place. Wouldn't it have been better for us to have Him with us here on earth? Imagine if you could schedule an appointment to go see Jesus! He could clear up all doctrinal disputes and answer every question in the Church once and for all. But Jesus had a better plan. Look at what He said in John 16:7: "Nevertheless I tell you the truth, it is to your advantage that I go away; for if I do not go away, the Helper will not come to you; but if I depart, I will send Him to you". John 14:16 and 15:26 both confirm for us that the Helper (*parakletos* – Advocate, Comforter, Counselor) is the Holy Spirit.

Jesus thought it would be better that He go away and the Holy Spirit come instead. That means that our current situation is the best-case scenario in terms of our relationship with God. If Jesus was here in the body, He could speak to us, but He would be on the outside. Of the Holy Spirit, Jesus said, "he dwells with you and will be in you" (John 14:17). Jesus upgraded "God With Us" to "God In Us" by His Ascension.

The Holy Spirit is involved at every point of our salvation. He draws us towards God, He convicts us of our sins, He activates our faith, He regenerates our souls, and He seals us for salvation. After that He sanctifies us by shaping us into Christ's image; He illuminates the Word so that we can understand it; He empowers our prayer, and enables a relationship between us and God. And He empowers us with His own limitless might. That's what Jesus meant by "your advantage" when He went away.

Jesus Himself did not do a lick of ministry or a single miracle until the Spirit came upon Him at His baptism (Luke 3:22). Every mighty work He did was by the power of the Holy Spirit. He led Him throughout His life, even to the cross, and then raised Him from the dead. Then when Jesus ascended to Heaven, He sent His Holy Spirit to do the same thing for His Church (Romans 8:11). By the Spirit we are able to experience the same life that Jesus lived.

This is why Jesus told the disciples not to begin their mission until the Spirit had come. "Behold, I send the Promise of My Father upon you; but tarry in the city of

Jerusalem until you are endued with power from on high" (Luke 24:49). Moments before His Ascension, Jesus was still directing their attention to the coming Helper: "But you will receive power when the Holy Spirit has come upon you, and you will be my witnesses in Jerusalem and in all Judea and Samaria, and to the end of the earth" (Acts 1:8). Then in Acts 2, the Holy Spirit came upon the Church in glorious power, with a rushing wind and tongues of fire – sent by the Ascended Jesus. And the rest of Acts reads as a greatest hits of the Holy Spirit at work through the Church.

Does this apply to you? You bet it does. Peter said, "The promise [of the Holy Spirit] is for you and for your children and for all who are far off, everyone whom the Lord our God calls to himself" (Acts 2:39). I hope that excites you, because it means that what Jesus had is available to you. God does not want you stumbling and struggling through life. We are to be "more than conquerors" (Romans 8:37), not powerless POW's! If you have put your faith in Jesus, then the Holy Spirit lives within you. You must learn to submit to His influence and seek His power. God desires for the resurrection power of the Spirit to course through you, for rivers of living water to flow out of your heart (John 7:37-39).

But how do you receive that gift? It's very simple – you ask! Jesus said, "If you then, who are evil, know how to give good gifts to your children, how much more will the heavenly Father give the Holy Spirit to those who ask him!" (Luke 11:13).

Now, some folks want to get pedantic about terminology and act as if you should not bother God by asking for "more love, more power", as we sing sometimes. But the early Church certainly did not have that problem. In Acts 4, after their first arrest, the apostles gathered the Church to pray. They prayed for boldness and they prayed for miracles, and God shook the building where they were praying. "And they were all filled with the Holy Spirit" (Acts 4:31). Can you be filled with the Spirit more than once? Apparently so! At the very least, God will not despise the prayer of a Christian crying out for more dynamic Holy Ghost fire. That's why Jesus ascended, remember? So that we could have a Helper on the inside.

DIRECTING THE CHURCH

This section is tied to the one before it. We focused just now on the personal side of the Holy Spirit's work. Jesus sends Him to activate salvation and empower holiness in every individual Christian. But there is a corporate aspect to this as well. Jesus is now directing the Church by that same Holy Spirit. As Colossians 1:18 says, "He is the head of the body, the church".

The Church is the worldwide family of the saved. We

have the same Savior, bought with the same blood. We therefore all have the same Father, which makes us brothers and sisters. And we have all been filled with the same Holy Spirit. That's a unity that no human organization could ever hope to achieve. We are all one, and we all have the same commission: to go into the world and make disciples (Matthew 28:19). In Heaven, Jesus has the perspective and power to oversee and direct the operations of the Church.

The New Testament uses a number of metaphors to describe the Church: a building, a Bride, and more. But one of Paul's favorites is the image of a body. You've heard this before – the Body of Christ. "For just as the body is one and has many members, and all the members of the body, though many, are one body, so it is with Christ" (1 Corinthians 12:12). Each person in the Church is necessary in order for us to be a true representative of Christ on the earth. Jesus is not here personally, but we are the hands and feet of Jesus when we live as He would and do as He directs.

Of course, none of us can live up to that standard. We are forgiven, but we are still petty, selfish and immature. So in order to shape us into the Church He needs, Jesus has commissioned the Holy Spirit to sanctify us. And He does that through what the Bible calls spiritual gifts.

Ephesians 4 specifically ties the giving of the spiritual gifts to the Ascension, and identifies the goal of these gifts as the maturity of the Church: "Grace was given to each one of us according to the measure of Christ's gift. Therefore it says, 'When he ascended on high he led a host of captives, and he gave gifts to men.' (In saying, 'He ascended,' what does it mean but that he has also descended into the lower regions, the earth? He who descended is the one who also ascended far above all the heavens, that he might fill all things.) And he gave the apostles, the prophets, the evangelists, the shepherds and teachers, to equip the saints for the work of ministry, for building up the body of Christ, until we all attain to the unity of the faith and of the knowledge of the Son of God, to mature manhood, to the measure of the stature of the fullness of Christ." (Ephesians 4:7-13)

Jesus ascended and gave gifts, like those of a prophet or an evangelist, to equip the saints for ministry. The leaders of the Church have been given their ministry so that they can help the others in the Church live out their ministry. Each person has a special supernatural gift from Jesus by the Holy Spirit. The Bible gives us numerous lists of these (1 Corinthians 12, Romans 12, 1 Peter 4), ranging from administration and encouragement to prophecy, healing and speaking in tongues.

Every one of these exists to build up the Body. It is the grace of God at work, which is why they are called the *charismata* ("gifts", from the word *charis*, meaning "grace"). When you use your spiritual gift, by helping another or teaching a Bible study, you become a channel of God's grace into that person's life. They are sanctified by the work that you do in the Spirit. That is God's plan to make disciples and grow up the Church. And that is what Jesus does from Heaven: He directs His people individually to work corporately so that we can have a universal impact for His Kingdom.

The danger comes when we stop listening to Jesus. We quench the Spirit, we ignore His Word, and we forget about God. People use the Church for their own benefit and promotion, or to advance their own ideas and social agendas. When man is head of Christ's Church, it fades into something less than what He intended. But no one can change what the Church really is. We all build on the foundation, but the foundation is only ever Jesus Christ. And some day you will be called to account for what you added to the Church. For some Christians, their work will be wood, hay and straw, burned up in the crucible of Heaven. Their lives will have counted for next to nothing, although their souls will be saved. But others will see their work refined into gold, silver and precious stones at the Judgment Seat of Christ (1 Corinthians 3:11-15). Jesus might be directing things from Heaven now, where you can't see Him, but make no mistake, He is watching. And someday we will all give an account for how we have acted in His Church.

So then – "Speaking the truth in love, we are to grow up in every way into him who is the head, into Christ, from whom the whole body, joined and held together by every joint with which it is equipped, when each part is working properly, makes the body grow so that it builds itself up in love" (Ephesians 4:15-16). When we all work together in spiritual harmony, we begin to look more like Jesus. Then our work on earth truly is an extension and continuation of His work, directed by Him from His Father's right hand.

WAITING FOR HIS RETURN

The final events of Jesus' life are often put together under one name: Exaltation. From the Kenosis to the Incarnation and the Crucifixion, Jesus underwent humiliation on our behalf. But the Resurrection, the Ascension and the Session of Christ are the first three parts of His Exaltation. There is one more: His Return.

Hebrews 10:12-13 explains: "But when Christ had offered for all time a single sacrifice for sins, he sat down at the right hand of God, waiting from that time until his enemies should be made a footstool for his feet". That is the fifth thing that Jesus does in Heaven – He is waiting for His return.

That reference to enemies as a footstool comes from Psalm 110:1. We've referred to Psalm 110 a few times. The primary theme of that song is the rule and victory of the Messiah. As the Son of David, Jesus has claim to the throne of Israel, and as the Son of God, He has claim to the whole world. He has not exercised that right yet. The kingdoms of this world are not yet the kingdoms our Lord and of His Christ (Revelation 11:15). But they will be! Everything that He has by right as the Son of God He will come to claim in fact.

Jesus waits in Heaven, directing His Church, interceding for us, but waiting, always waiting for the day when He shall return. He told the disciples that even He does not know when it will be (Mark 13:32). We experience the Kingdom of God in our hearts, that "foretaste of glory divine", but there is no Kingdom on this earth – yet. Someday, the fullness of the Church will be brought in. And then the end will come.

First, Christ will come to rescue His Church. He said at the Last Supper, "In my Father's house are many rooms. If it were not so, would I have told you that I go to prepare a place for you? And if I go to prepare a place for you, I will come again and will take you to myself, that where I am you may be also" (John 14:2-3). We understand the "going away" part, that's the Ascension. But He says that He will come to take us to His Father's house; that is, of course, in Heaven. We call this the Rapture, from the Latin *raptura*, meaning to "snatch, carry away". 1 Corinthians 15:51-54 and 1 Thessalonians 4:15-17 tell us that the living and dead Church will be "caught up" into Heaven to be with Christ forever. And it is only then that God will pour out His wrath on the world. He could not do that with us here, because the wrath of God for us was satisfied at the cross (1 Thessalonians 5:9). Like a bridegroom returning for His bride, Jesus will return to take us to be with Him in Heaven.

Second, Christ will come to redeem Israel. The Bible prophesies seven years of Tribulation, when God removes His restraining hand (2 Thessalonians 2:7). A wicked man called the Antichrist will set up a false kingdom, and all will be made to worship him. He will bring peace at first, but then he will turn a violent hand to the Jews and those who come to believe on Jesus during that time. And the Lord will rock the world with plagues and curses and demonic hordes and stars falling from Heaven. Jerusalem will be surrounded, the Jews about to be annihilated. Then, as the Lord says in Zechariah 12:10, "I will pour out on the house of David and the inhabitants of Jerusalem a spirit of grace and pleas for mercy, so that, when they look on me, on him whom they have pierced, they shall mourn for him, as one mourns for an only child, and weep bitterly over him, as one weeps for a firstborn". Israel will finally recognize Jesus as the Messiah, fulfilling the ultimatum of Matthew 23:39.

Third and finally, Christ will come to exercise retribution against evil. Revelation 19:11-16 describes Jesus not as a peaceful carpenter, but a conquering King, splattered with the blood of His enemies, striking down the nations in fierce wrath. As the angels prophesied in Acts 1, Jesus will return to the Mount of Olives – from where He ascended – and it will split in two at the glory of His coming (Zechariah 14:4). He will destroy the ungodly armies of the Antichrist, He will judge the nations in righteousness, and Satan will be bound for 1,000 years. Then begins the Millennial Reign of Jesus. This is the final stage in His Exaltation. From the manger and the grave to the sky and the throne.

Think of the anticipation! Jesus is waiting for the word from His Father that all has been made ready. And every day He knows that we are closer than the day before. Do you not feel the same delicious suspense? At any moment, you might hear the trumpet and be called up yonder to be with Christ forever. So, as John said, "abide in him, so that when he appears we may have confidence and not shrink from him in shame at his coming" (1 John 2:28). Let's live every moment as if "it might be today" – because it just might be.

CONCLUSION

We've seen that the Ascension is a biblical priority, foretold in the Old Testament, during Jesus' life, and after

His Resurrection. We looked at the mechanics of the Ascension, that Jesus ascended bodily to Heaven, in permanent Hypostatic Union with humanity. And we looked in detail at His ongoing work in Heaven today: (1) He is mediating our salvation, (2) He is interceding on our behalf, (3) He is sending His Holy Spirit, (4) He is directing His Church, and (5) He is waiting for His return.

I hope you've been able to see that the Ascension is not an afterthought, but the capstone of the mission of the Son. All that remains now is the consummation of all things. In the meantime, though, Christ has work to do, and so do you. The truth of the Ascension ought to put spurs to our lives here on earth. "If then you have been raised with Christ, seek the things that are above, where Christ is, seated at the right hand of God. Set your minds on things that are above, not on things that are on earth. For you have died, and your life is hidden with Christ in God. When Christ who is your life appears, then you also will appear with him in glory" (Colossians 3:1-4).

Read those verses again, they are truly magnificent! It reminds us of our solidarity with Christ Jesus. We are "in Him" the New Testament says repeatedly. Our lives are to be mirrors of His. We die to sin and rise to walk in newness of life (Romans 6:5). Ephesians 2:6 says we are "seated...with him in the heavenly places". And someday, we shall return with Him in glory, to rule and reign with

Him on the earth (Revelation 20:6).

Because Jesus has taken humanity with Him into Heaven, you and I share that same destiny through faith. We will always retain our subordinate, creaturely relationship to the Lord, but we share not just in the death and resurrection, but even the exaltation of Jesus. By faith we are united with Christ, and Christ is united with God. You have been brought into the very family of the Godhead itself. Salvation is participation in Christ, and His Ascension is what solidifies that truth.

If all this is so, how can we allow ourselves to be distracted by vain frivolities? Offer a millionaire a scratch-off lottery ticket and he'll laugh in your face. Why would he be tempted by something so cheap? The same is true for you and me. My Jesus is at His Father's right hand, and I have been brought into fellowship with Him. There is nothing left to tempt me or intimidate me or frighten me or entice me. I sing with all the saints who sang it before me:

"Give me Jesus! Give me Jesus!

You can have all this world, just give me Jesus!"

Conclusion

His Final Days

I love the way that last chapter ends. "You can have all this world, just give me Jesus!" I didn't write those words, of course, but it is the cry of my heart. And I hope that after reading about His final days, it's the cry of your heart too.

That's what this book is all about. We discussed history and theology and heard some interesting stories, but in the end it's all about Jesus. If there's one thing to draw from this book, it is that Jesus is worthy of your entire life. Knowing what we know about who He is and what He's done, how foolish would we be to relegate Him to the sidelines of our hearts?

If you are a Christian, be reminded of what that means. It's not just a cute cultural identifier. That name means something. It means that you have died to your old life and are living a new one for His glory and by His power (Galatians 2:20). Maybe you are doing well. In that case, I hope this book has increased your knowledge and your joy. Maybe you are a backslider. I hope this has reignited the fire in your heart. Maybe you are neither, you're just hurt and broken. I hope the truth of the Gospel has brought peace and healing to your life. Let Jesus be the center, Christian, and everything else will fall into place.

But if you have read this book and you know that you are on the outside, that you are not one of Christ's disciples, but a lost soul – then I've got Good News for you!

Jesus Christ was not just another man. He was the eternal Son of God. He came to live as a man so that He could die for your sins. The wrong things you have done, and the character that produces those things, is worthy of eternal death in Hell. But Jesus died on the cross as a perfect substitute so that I could make this offer to you: If you cry out to God, ask for His forgiveness and invoke the name of Christ as your hope, then you will be saved! The death of Jesus can count for you if you will only ask. If you continue in pride and self-sufficiency, then Hell awaits for you. But why would you do that? I'm offering you the free gift of abundant life now and eternal life in Heaven later! All you need to do is ask. God is listening. He's waiting to forgive your sins, change your heart and turn your life around.

And I'm praying for you too, for all of you! If you were blessed, or if you have questions, please get in touch, I would be delighted to hear from you.

"Now to him who is able to keep you from stumbling and to present you blameless before the presence of his glory with great joy, to the only God, our Savior, through Jesus Christ our Lord, be glory, majesty, dominion, and authority, before all time and now and forever. Amen." (Jude 24-25)

THANKS FOR READING!

For more resources from Pastor Tyler Warner, including free eBooks, recorded Bible teachings, and devotional videos, visit CalvaryChapelTrussville.com.

To connect with Calvary Chapel Trussville, you can check Facebook, Instagram and YouTube for regular uploads.

And if you were blessed by this book, please get in touch with us and let us know. We'd be delighted to know you!

Calvary Chapel Trussville

5239 Old Springville Rd, Pinson, AL, 35126
CalvaryChapelTrussville.com
Office@CalvaryChapelTrussville.com

Made in the USA
Columbia, SC
09 May 2021

37118474R00113